Thoughts of a Simple Man

in a

Complicated World

Jim Williams

THOUGHTS OF A Simple Man IN A COMPLICATED WORLD

Faith, Failure, and the Quiet Work of Redemption

Jim Williams

Jim Williams

Thoughts of a Simple Man in a Complicated World
Faith, Failure, and the Quiet Work of Redemption

Scripture quotations are from the Holy Bible, English Standard Version® (ESV®), © 2001 Crossway.
Used by permission. All rights reserved.

This book reflects the author's personal experiences and opinions and is not intended as theological, legal, medical, psychological, or professional advice. Readers are encouraged to seek qualified counsel and engage in Scripture prayerfully in forming their own conclusions.

First Edition, 2026

Published by
Porch Light Publishing
An imprint of Porch Light Reflections LLC

www.porchlightreflections.com

ISBN: 979-8-99575-712-2 (paperback)

Library of Congress Control Number: 2026910517

Printed in the United States of America

Dedication

First and foremost, to the Lord —
the Author of my faith and the steady hand
that has guided every step of this journey.

To my wife, Linnie —
for your patience, strength, and love
that steadies this Simple Man more than you know.

To my children, Austin and Katelyn,
my stepchildren, Marc, Sebastian, Mason, and Byron,
and my grandchildren, Luna, Axel, and Bentley —
may you walk with courage, seek truth with humility,
and never be afraid to ask hard questions.

To Jennifer —
though you are my cousin, you are, in every way that matters, my
sister.
Thank you for your love, your loyalty,
and the bond that life itself could never weaken.

To my grandmother —
who took me in at thirteen months old
and raised me with a strong foundation,
teaching me that faith, hard work, and love
are the pillars a life must stand on.

To Blaine Mullis —
my old bus partner and catalyst,
whose encouragement led me to Liberty University
and opened the door to a bachelor's and a master's.

And to my friends, family, and church family
who have walked beside me along the way —
thank you for your conversations, correction, laughter, and grace.

Contents

"Iron sharpens iron,

and one man sharpens another."

— Proverbs 27:17 (ESV)

From the Porch

There's something about a front porch. It's where conversations slow down, where stories get told, where you don't have to have everything figured out—you just have to be willing to sit for a while.

This book was never meant to be complicated. Honestly… it was never meant to be perfect either.

It came from quiet moments, from questions I didn't always have answers to, from life as it really is—messy, meaningful, and sometimes hard to understand.

Some of these thoughts were written in the middle of long days. Some came from looking back on things I've lived through. And some came from simply sitting still long enough to notice what God was already doing.

If you're holding this edition in your hands, I want you to know something… this one matters to me.

Not because it's polished or complete—but because it's personal. Every copy has been handled, signed, and sent out with intention.

Wherever you are right now, whether life feels steady or uncertain—my hope is simple:

That somewhere in these pages, you'll find a moment to pause. To breathe. To reflect.

And when you finally put this book down, I hope it feels like we've been sitting on the porch together for a while… and maybe you find yourself thinking, "He gets me."

And more than that— "I don't feel so alone anymore."

There's always room on the porch.

Foreword

"I am not where I imagined I'd be several years ago. Not even close. If you had told the younger version of me—the one who barely made it out of high school, the one who failed English, the one who had to sit through summer school just to pass—that one day he would be attending Liberty University at fifty-four years old, I would have laughed. If you had told me I'd begin working on a master's degree at fifty-six, I would have shaken my head. And if you had told me that someday someone would be holding a book with my name on it—words I wrote—I would have said, 'You've got the wrong guy.'"

The above quote by our author, Jim Williams, reminded me of a Bible verse penned by the Apostle Paul in Ephesians 3:20:

"Now to him who is able to do immeasurably more than all we ask or imagine, according to his power that is at work within us." (NIV)

Our Heavenly Father loves to do incredible things in the lives of His children who are humbly surrendered and obedient to Him.

I had the pleasure of meeting Jim back in late 2022, just after my retirement from a long career as an insurance fraud investigator. Upon retiring, I learned from a prior coworker that there was a shortage of school bus drivers in my local public school district. With newfound time, I obtained the required credentials and training to become a school bus driver and was assigned to drive a bus for exceptional children. Shortly afterward, Jim was appointed as the monitor on my bus transportation safety assistant.

Little did either of us know this was a providential assignment. God had a plan and a purpose to cross our paths.

We quickly discovered we had many shared interests, but more importantly, we were kindred spirits—brothers in Christ. We talked often about our faith. I shared my testimony, where I had surrendered my life to Christ back in 1990 after having been raised in church and spending 28 years "playing church." Upon being saved, I became an avid reader of the Bible and Christian material, which eventually led me to teach Sunday school.

Jim shared his testimony as well—the very journey you will read about in this book.

Each morning before our bus route, we would pray—for the children, their parents, our coworkers, our families—and that our lives would bring honor and glory to our Lord and Savior, Jesus Christ. We spoke often about growing deeper in our relationship with Him, even exploring Hebrew and Greek for a clearer understanding of Scripture.

We also discussed the spiritual and practical "thoughts" Jim would share—many of which would later become part of this book. I was always impressed by the wisdom and honesty in his words. It was clear God had gifted "Big Jim" with a voice worth hearing.

One day, Jim told me his wife had volunteered him to teach preschool and early elementary children at the Wednesday night Bible study. He admitted he felt completely unprepared. I told him the truth—this is the very group most people avoid, but he was exactly who God would use. Almost immediately, his demeanor changed. The Holy Spirit filled him with peace and gave him the courage to step out of his comfort zone and walk forward in faith.

Jim may give me credit as a catalyst in his journey, but I believe it was in that moment—when he said "yes" to God—that everything shifted. Teaching those young, impressionable minds the Word of God became the launching point for something greater.

I watched my brother in Christ grow spiritually right there on that bus route. I often told him, "God has big plans for you, brother—just wait and see." And over the past several years, I have witnessed something only God could orchestrate.

This Holy Spirit-inspired fervor is what led to the writing of this book.

This book is a must-read—whether you take it one "thought" at a time as a daily devotional or read it in one sitting. Either way, you will be inspired, encouraged, and blessed.

You may be reminded of the innocence and reflection of Forrest Gump, or the small-town honesty of The Andy Griffith Show, but what you will find here carries something deeper spiritual weight and eternal purpose.

Jim candidly shares his life story—from humble beginnings in rural North Carolina near the Outer Banks, through the highs and lows of adulthood, into the fast-paced world of NASCAR racing, where—of all places—he encountered redemption and salvation. From there, his path leads to earning not one, but two Bachelor of Science degrees from Liberty University, with plans to pursue a master's degree.

These pages are filled with "thoughts," "stakes in the ground," and "sparks"—moments that mark the journey of a life being shaped by God.

Jim often speaks of "the porch"—a place where truth lives. A place where conversations unfold without pretense. Where neighbors lean back in wooden chairs, laughter mixes with wisdom, and stories are shared freely without microphones or platforms. The porch carries a sacred honesty.

And that is exactly what you will find in this book.

You will encounter raw, unashamed honesty—failures, breakthroughs, struggles, and victories—all woven together by the truth that "God wastes nothing."

Romans 8:28 reminds us:

"And we know that in all things God works for the good of those who love him, who have been called according to his purpose." (NIV)

Jeremiah 29:11 declares:

"For I know the plans I have for you," says the Lord, "plans to prosper you and not to harm you, plans to give you hope and a future." (NIV)

And Psalm 37:23 assures us:

"The steps of a man are established by the Lord, when he delights in his way." (ESV)

Enjoy the read.

You will be blessed.

Blaine Mullis

Come Up On Porch

This isn't a theological textbook, and it isn't a collection of polished answers neatly tied with certainty. It is simply a man — a simple man — trying to make sense of faith while living in a world that rarely feels simple. If you find yourself disagreeing with some of my conclusions, remember that is all they are — conclusions, opinions formed along the road of lived experience. And if something here unsettles you or even offends you, perhaps this book wasn't written for you. But then again… maybe it was. Sometimes the conversations we resist are the ones we need most.

I've wanted to write a book for a long time, though I never quite knew what it would be about or whether anyone would ever read it. There was just this quiet itch in me — a sense that maybe the twists, setbacks, victories, and detours of life weren't random after all. Maybe they carried meaning. I'm not writing because I've figured life out. I haven't. I've wrecked things. Lost things. Started over more times than I care to count. I've been the man who looked steady on the outside while quietly coming undone on the inside. But I've also witnessed God show up in places I never expected, in moments I never could have planned. And at its heart, that's what this story is really about.

My name is James Robert Williams Jr. Back home, they still call me Jimmy, though most folks today simply say, "Jim". I'm a big fella, the kind of person people sometimes assume is intimidating until I start talking. Truth is, I've always just been a thinking man. I enjoy deep conversations. I enjoy wrestling with questions.

I enjoy talking about God — even when the answers aren't clean or comfortable.

For much of my life, I knew about God far more than I knew Him. And there's a difference between awareness and relationship that only becomes clear with time.

I was raised by my grandmother in a small town where life didn't follow what most would call a traditional path. My parents weren't truly present in the day-to-day shaping of my world, but love was never absent. My grandmother made certain of that. My Aunt Jerrie used to joke, "He's mine — he just didn't come with the birth pains." That line stayed with me because it taught me something early: family isn't defined by structure alone. It's defined by presence, commitment, and love that shows up.

My childhood unfolded in creeks, woods, and dusty roads alongside a group of boys we proudly called the Oakum Street Outlaws. We didn't spend much time worrying about danger or consequences. We simply lived. Fishing lines cast into quiet water. Football games on the courthouse green. Laughter stretched long past sunset. Those were good days — simple days before life gathered speed.

As the years rolled forward, life naturally grew louder. I became a firefighter in my hometown, a calling that shapes a man in ways hard to explain. When you stand beside people in their worst moments, perspective changes. You learn what matters; you learn what doesn't. Yet I've always carried a restless streak. I chased opportunities that pulled me across states and into new chapters. Eventually, that road led me to Hendrick Motorsports — a world of roaring engines, precision, pressure, and organized chaos. It felt like an arrival. Until it didn't.

Losing that job struck deeper than I anticipated. When something entwines itself with your identity and is suddenly taken away, the silence afterward can feel deafening. You begin asking questions that refuse to be ignored.

Who am I without this? What remains when the title disappears? That season forced reflection I might otherwise have avoided.

Life handed me failures along the way — marriages that didn't last, decisions I regret, moments that wounded others, and moments that wounded me. There were stretches where doubt crept in quietly, where confidence thinned, where direction blurred. And somewhere in the middle of that long, uneven road, I encountered Jesus in a way I never had before. Not the distant figure of childhood stories. Not the Sunday-morning-only presence. But the Christ who sits with you in wreckage and does not leave. That shift didn't fix everything overnight, nor did it make me flawless. But it changed my direction. And direction changes everything.

At fifty-four years old — an age when many men consider slowing down — I found myself stepping back into classrooms. Not out of boredom, nor ambition, nor a need to prove something to the world, but from a stirring I couldn't shake. Today, I stand one semester away from completing two bachelor's degrees — one in Biblical Studies and Theology, the other in Next Gen Ministries. And just when I might have been expected to pause, another step opened ahead. This fall, I begin pursuing a Master's in Art of Teaching with a specialty in Special Education. None of that feels glamorous. It feels like obedience.

Growth rarely looks impressive from the inside.
Most of the time, it looks like late nights, second guesses, persistence, and trust.

This book isn't truly about racing, though racing gave me language for understanding life. In racing, the pits are where adjustments happen — where broken things are repaired, strategies reconsidered, and breath regained before returning to the noise.

When I look back, many of my defining moments happened there — not necessarily on tracks, but in those life "pits" where direction shifted and clarity emerged.

If you're reading this and you feel like you're standing in one of those places — uncertain, paused, recalibrating — perhaps these pages will remind you the race isn't finished. I'm not ahead of you. I'm not above you.

I'm simply a man who has spun out a few times and found God standing faithfully when the smoke cleared. And if anything written here helps you feel less alone on your own road, then every lap, every detour, every pit stop was worth it.

Let's walk this thing together.

The Man on the Porch

I never grew up imagining I would one day write anything down. I was raised in northeastern North Carolina, where the land lies flat and the sandy soil stretches toward a horizon wide enough to cradle both dreams and doubts. The Chowan River winds quietly in one direction, the Albemarle Sound opens wide in another, and the wind seems to carry more than the scent of water — it carries memory, heritage, and stories whispered through generations. In that part of the world, life teaches long before books ever try. Patience looks like waiting on crops. Storms arrive without asking permission. Faith is absorbed through lived example more often than spoken instruction. Life rarely pauses to explain itself. It simply unfolded, and you learned to stand steady within it.

When I call myself a "Simple Man," I don't mean my life has been simple. Far from it. I mean, I've come to understand that complicated answers rarely mend complicated hearts. The world today feels loud in ways it never used to. Politics shout. Religion debates. Social media churns endlessly with opinions, arguments, and noise. Yet most of the people I've known — good, hardworking, sincere people — are simply trying to make sense of it all. I'm no different. I've wrestled with questions in church pews and worked through thoughts on quiet front porches. I've answered altar calls and carried private doubts. I've learned what it means to love Jesus while sometimes struggling to understand His people. I've seen faith serve as a bridge that brings healing, and I've seen it wielded as a weapon that wounds.

Over time, one truth settled gently but firmly in my spirit: the quiet voice often travels farther than the loud one.
And for me, the porch has always been the place where that truth lives as a boy, and now as a man. The porch was where conversations unfolded, and life was sorted without spectacle. It was where neighbors leaned back in worn wooden chairs, where laughter mixed with wisdom, where stories passed freely without microphones or platforms. I can still picture my grandmother sitting there for hours, speaking life in ways she likely never realized, shaping hearts through presence more than persuasion. The porch held a kind of sacredness — not because it was grand, but because it was honest.

That's what this book is meant to be. Not a sermon series. Not a political manifesto. Not a collection of polished arguments designed to impress. This is a porch — a place to speak plainly about the stakes in the ground, the defining moments that shaped me, steadied me, saved me, and at times nearly broke me. When I look back across the years, I don't see a neat, straight path. I see moments — quiet intersections where decisions were made, where grace arrived, where life changed direction. And one of those moments came on a night I never saw coming.

So, before you turn the page, pull up a chair. Let the screen door creak softly behind you. Imagine a glass of iced tea sweating in the Carolina heat. Sit for a while.

And let me tell you about the first stake in the ground.

The Night That Changed Everything

The first stake in the ground didn't happen inside a church, at least not at first. It began in a race shop, in a world defined by grease under the fingernails, the sharp scent of fuel and rubber hanging in the air, and tools scattered across worn workbenches. That was the environment I understood. Performance mattered there. Precision mattered. Results mattered. Everything had a measurable outcome. And right in the middle of that ordinary, fast-paced world, a co-worker did something that seemed small at the time — he invited me to church. There was no debate, no pressure, no sermon tucked into the invitation. Just a simple, genuine offer. Looking back now, I can see it clearly: some of the most important stakes in life are driven quietly, without spectacle or ceremony.

That evening, the pastor spoke about Nicodemus — a man who, on the surface, had it all together. He was religious, respected, knowledgeable, yet still drawn to Jesus under the cover of night, carrying questions he couldn't silence. When the pastor read Jesus' words, "You must be born again," John 3:3 (ESV), something in me shifted. Not improved. Not adjusted. Not cleaned up. Born again. Those words didn't feel like distant theology. They felt personal. Nicodemus stopped being just a figure from Scripture; he became a mirror. Put together on the outside, restless and empty on the inside. That was me. I had believed in God. I had respected Him. But I was still firmly in the driver's seat of my own life, gripping the wheel, trusting my own control.

And then it happened — not with drama, not with thunder, but with a quiet clarity that left no room for doubt.

A gentle tug at my shirt. Invisible, yet undeniable. A voice, not heard through my ears but settled deeply in my spirit, steady and unmistakable: "It's time." Time to stop pretending. Time to stop performing. Time to surrender. That moment became the first true stake in the ground. I walked out of that church the same man in appearance — same job, same responsibilities, same life waiting for me — yet something fundamental had changed. A race team invitation had quietly become a rescue mission. A sermon about Nicodemus had become a reflection of my own condition. A simple tug at my shirt had become the place where heaven intersected my timeline.

It was October 2008. Life was loud, filled with engines, deadlines, and tires screaming across asphalt. I had grown up hearing the stories of Jesus — tent revivals, river baptisms, altar calls — but I had never stepped fully into that story myself. I had spent years searching, often in the dark, often without knowing exactly what I was looking for. But that night, I stepped forward. My coworkers prayed with me. Something shifted deep within me. Life didn't suddenly become smooth or simple. There were still struggles, still questions, still seasons that tested me in ways I never expected. But that night — the night I found God in the middle of the race — laid a foundation strong enough to carry me through all of it. And from that moment forward, nothing, absolutely nothing, has ever been the same.

Redemption in a Complicated World

The next morning still came, just like it always does. There was no halo, no sudden perfection, no dramatic outward transformation waiting for me when my feet hit the floor — just the familiar sound of the alarm clock and the same life calling me back into its routines. And yet, beneath the ordinary surface of that morning, something had undeniably shifted. Before that night, faith had been something I respected, something I believed in from a careful distance. After that night, it became something I belonged to. Redemption did not erase my past, nor did it rewind consequences or instantly repair what had been broken. What it gave me instead was something far more powerful: a new direction. And direction, I've learned, has a way of changing everything. Grace does not cancel your past; it confronts it honestly, and then — somehow — walks you forward anyway. That realization became another defining moment in my life, not loud or emotional, but steady, grounding, and deeply personal.

Life, however, has never stopped reminding me how complicated this world can feel. Some days, everything seems to move faster than my heart can comfortably process. Chaos grows loudly. Brokenness becomes visible. Uncertainty presses in from directions I didn't anticipate. In moments like that, it's easy for a man to feel small, unsettled, even slightly adrift. But when I open my Bible, I encounter something different. I found a quiet place. A steady voice. A reminder that God has not surrendered His authority to the noise of the world. Reading Genesis 6 recently,

I was struck again by the sobering description of humanity — that the Lord saw the wickedness of man was great upon the earth, that every inclination of the human heart leaned toward evil. It's a heavy picture, one that mirrors more of our present reality than we sometimes care to admit. Yet right there, in the center of that darkness, Scripture offers a simple but powerful contrast: Noah found favor in the eyes of the Lord. Not because he was flawless. Not because he was extraordinary by human standards. But because he chose to trust God when everything around him moved in the opposite direction.

That truth does not remain trapped in ancient history. It stretches forward into our lives today. The world may feel fractured, loud, and uncertain, but God's redemptive pattern has not changed. Just as He made a way for Noah, He has made a way for us through Jesus Christ. John 3:16 continues to echo with steady hope — that God so loved the world He gave His Son, that whoever believes would not perish but have eternal life. And so, I keep learning this lesson slowly and imperfectly: when darkness seems to surround us, grace remains. When the world feels unstable, hope is still available. We are not left to navigate chaos alone. God has already made a way.

Maybe, then, the invitation is simpler than we often make it. Pause. Breathe. Remember who holds the story. Turn toward Him again. Trust Him again. And live, day by day, in a way that reflects even a small measure of His light in this complicated world.

Tree on the Mountain

I've said this before in these pages, and if I'm being honest, it's a lesson I keep circling back to. I have a real struggle with identity. Not the surface-level kind, but the deeper questions that creep in when life gets quiet. Questions about being good enough, about measuring up, about belonging. I don't know exactly where that root was planted. Maybe it traces back to when my mom and dad gave me up. Maybe somewhere inside, a little boy decided he'd spend the rest of his life trying to prove he was worth keeping. My grandmother loved me with a steadiness that still humbles me, but even wrapped in that love, there has always been this whisper in the background — that uneasy feeling that my place must somehow be earned.

That old tension followed me even into places where you'd think it would finally go silent. I was back at Quest, serving on the ministry team at Joy Mountain in North Carolina — a place that, to me, feels like God's country. That mountain holds sacred ground in my story. It's where I wrestled. Where the Lord met me in hard, refining moments. Now I was returning not as a participant, but as staff, helping other men walk through battles that looked a lot like my own. You'd think standing in the middle of ministry would quiet those identity questions. Sometimes it does. Sometimes it doesn't.

One afternoon, I found myself standing at a window, looking out over the mountainside. The view was breathtaking — rolling hills blanketed in deep green, trees bursting with life, color, fullness. But there, tucked among all that green, stood one lone tree. Bare. Brown. No leaves. Just standing there by itself.

And before I could stop it, the thought slipped quietly into my mind: That's you. You don't fit. It wasn't loud. Lies rarely are. It didn't thunder; it whispered. You're different. You don't blend. You don't belong in this life. I stood there staring, seconds away from letting that thought settle into something heavier. That's the dangerous thing about deception — it often sounds like your own voice.

A brother from the ministry team noticed me standing there and walked over. "Hey," he asked gently, "what are you doing?" I pointed toward the hillside. "See that tree?" I said. "That's me. I don't fit." He didn't laugh. Didn't correct me sharply. He simply looked out the window for a long moment. Then he said something that shifted the ground beneath that lie.

"No," he said quietly. "That's not you because you don't fit. That's you because you're set apart. All that green around it? That's the world. That tree isn't blending in — it's different on purpose."

I hadn't seen it that way. And isn't that just like the enemy? To take something born of purpose and twist it into isolation. Making a distinction feels like rejection. But Scripture tells a steadier story. We are called chosen, not misplaced. Set apart, not sidelined. Transformed, not conformed. Jesus Himself said that those who belong to Him would not always feel at home in the patterns of the world.

Still, let me be honest in the way porch conversations demand honesty — that truth doesn't automatically make the feeling disappear. It isn't always easy to walk into rooms and feel different. It isn't always easy to silence the voice that questions your worth. I know what it feels like to stand at windows believing lies about not belonging.

But God speaks differently. He calls us His workmanship. His adopted children. Accepted, not tolerated. The world may whisper, You don't fit. God says, You're set apart.

Maybe you've known that feeling too — like the lone tree in a forest of green. Maybe you've questioned whether you belong. I'm not writing this as a man who has mastered identity. I'm writing this as a man still learning, day by day, to believe what God says over what the lie suggests.

Standing there on Joy Mountain, I nearly believed I was out of place. But maybe — just maybe — the tree wasn't misplaced at all. Maybe it was planted exactly where it was meant to stand.

"Trust in the Lord with all your heart,

and do not lean on your own understanding.

In all your ways acknowledge him,

and he will make straight your paths."

— Proverbs 3:5–6 (ESV)

Believing, But Not Living It

I don't mind admitting this, though it may sound uncomfortable at first. There have been seasons in my life where the only honest description I could find was something like a "Christian atheist." Harsh words, maybe, but truth has a way of cutting clean. Especially after I first came to faith, I struggled to loosen my grip on the world. I knew the language of Christianity. I knew the verses, the songs, the rhythms. I showed up. From the outside, I looked like a man walking steadily with God. But there were days my living didn't quite match my believing.

I never doubted God's existence. That wasn't the problem. The tension lived somewhere deeper. I said He was Lord, yet I kept my hands tight on the steering wheel. I prayed, yet worried as though my prayers vanished into empty air. I sang about surrender while quietly guarding my own plans. It's a strange and dangerous place — believing the right things while keeping the heart partly anchored to the wrong ones. Faith can exist in the mind while hesitation lingers in the will.

Jesus' words to the church in Laodicea have always carried a weight that's hard to shake: "Because you are lukewarm — neither hot nor cold — I will spit you out of my mouth." Those words aren't directed at unbelievers standing outside the church walls. They're aimed squarely at those of us inside. Those who identify. Those who profess. Those who believe — but no longer burn. It's a sobering picture. Not comforting. Not softened. Just honest.

Drifting rarely feels dramatic when you're living it. No thunderclap announces the shift. No clear dividing line appears beneath your feet. It's gradual, almost polite. Edges soften. Convictions quiet. Obedience becomes negotiable. Comfort slowly replaces surrender. I've known those seasons — times when I loved Jesus yet still clung to pieces of the world more tightly than I wanted to admit. Times when I welcomed grace but resisted repentance. Wanted salvation without fully embracing transformation. That quiet "but" is where faith grows thin.

And so, the question that keeps circling my heart is not whether I believe in God, but whether I believe God. Believing in Him can be surprisingly inexpensive. Believing Him — trusting what He says about sin, obedience, surrender, holiness — that carries a cost. Sometimes a painful one. Sometimes everything. But perhaps that's where simple faith truly begins. Not in loud declarations or polished appearances, but in the quiet honesty of a heart laid bare before Him.

I know what it feels like to wrestle with identity. To not quite fit in. To feel pulled between two worlds. But the middle ground is not nearly as safe as it feels. A complicated world doesn't need more people who wear faith as a label while living as though God is distant. It needs men and women whose lives quietly testify that He is real, present, holy, watching, leading, and worth obeying.

I don't write this as someone who has mastered the walk. I write it as a simple man who has seen enough of his own weakness to know I don't want to gamble on lukewarm faith. Eternity is far too long, and grace far too precious, to live half awake.

Somewhere I Never Planned to Be

We don't always know what God has planned for us, and if I'm being honest, that truth has met me in more late-night prayers than I can count. I've asked Him directly, sometimes quietly, sometimes with frustration, sometimes with tears: "Lord, where is this going? What are you doing? Why doesn't this look anything like what I thought my life would be?" Because I can tell you this much — I am not where I imagined I'd be several years ago. Not even close. If you had told the younger version of me — the one who barely made it out of high school, the one who failed English, the one who had to sit through summer school just to pass — that one day he would be attending Liberty University at fifty-four years old, I would have laughed. If you had told me I'd begin working on a master's degree at fifty-six, I would have shaken my head. And if you had told me that someday someone would be holding a book with my name on it — words I wrote — I would have said, "You've got the wrong guy."

I wasn't the smart kid. I wasn't the polished kid. I failed English. Let that sink in. And yet, here you are reading sentences that somehow made their way through my hands. I'm an online student, not a traditional one. I didn't walk on campus at fifty-four; I logged into classes after work, after responsibilities, after life. Back then, I only cared about passing. Now I find myself disappointed if I make ninety. Truth be told, I'm glad I'm older doing this. I don't think I would have cared about this many years ago. If that doesn't speak to the patience and providence of God, I don't know what does.

Jeremiah reminds us that God says, "For I know the plans I have for you." Notice the emphasis there — I know, not you know. That verse isn't a promise that life will unfold predictably; it's a promise that it will unfold purposefully.

Proverbs tell us that humans plan their course, but the Lord establishes their steps. I had plans. God had steps. And His steps have led me places my plans never even considered. There were seasons when I fell behind, seasons when I thought I had missed my window, seasons when I quietly wondered if maybe I just wasn't capable of more. But what I'm learning at this stage of life is something steady and comforting: God wastes nothing. Not the years you think were lost. Not the failures that embarrassed you. Not the classes you barely passed. Not the doors that closed. He uses it all.

Sometimes, He simply waits until you're seasoned enough, humbled enough, steady enough to carry what He intends to give you. Starting college at fifty-four wasn't in my five-year plan. A master's degree certainly wasn't. Writing a book wasn't even on the radar. But obedience was. And obedience, I'm learning, is the part I can control. Be patient. Be faithful. Do what God places in front of you, even when it feels small or delayed. Because He can do exceedingly abundantly above all that we ask or think — above what we think. I didn't think this life chapter was possible. Yet here we are. And if you're reading this feeling behind, underqualified, or defined by past failures, let a simple man encourage you: I failed English, barely escaped high school, and God still wrote a different ending than I ever imagined. He's not finished with you either. Stay patient. Stay obedient. The Author may be writing a chapter you wouldn't have dared to dream.

Grace After the Wreckage

Surrender doesn't erase consequences, and that's a truth I've had to learn without shortcuts. Some apologies still had to be made. Some trust still had to be rebuilt. Some pride still had to be swallowed — not once, but daily. Grace is not God pretending the damage never happened. Grace is God walking beside you while you repair what you can and teaching you to trust Him with what you cannot. Healing, at least in my life, wasn't dramatic or cinematic. It was slow obedience. Choosing humility instead of ego. Choosing patience instead of reaction. Choosing truth instead of protecting an image. Those choices didn't feel like mountaintop moments; they felt like doing the right thing when it would have been easier not to. Yet those small decisions became stakes driven quietly into the ground, marking the slow reshaping of a man.

So, pull up a chair on the porch with me for a minute, because I want to talk to the man who's sitting there quietly, wondering if he's used up all his chances. I've had two failed marriages. The first marriage, that one sits squarely on my shoulders. I was a young firefighter married to a nurse. It looked perfect from the outside, like something out of a Norman Rockwell painting. But long shifts, immaturity, and an undisciplined heart can create cracks you don't notice until the structure gives way. I wandered into places I should never have gone and betrayed a woman who had done nothing wrong. That divorce belongs to me. The second relationship lasted more than twenty years, when you count both dating and marriage. We built a life. Shared experiences. Traveled through the NASCAR world.

Raised my son — the greatest earthly gift God has ever entrusted to me. From the church pew, we looked solid. But behind closed doors, silence and unspoken struggles slowly rotted the beams. That story carried weight on both sides. Now I'm married again, and I love this woman deeply. Loving her has stretched me, humbled me, and refined me. She's neurodivergent, and our life together is sometimes heavy, sometimes beautiful, and most days a mixture of both. And if you're the man asking, "Am I doomed because I've failed before?" let me tell you what I've learned the hard way.

First, own what's yours. God does not work with excuses nearly as well as He works with honesty. "The sacrifices of God are a broken spirit; a broken and contrite heart, O God, you will not despise." When I finally stopped explaining my failures and called them what they were, something shifted.

Repentance isn't weakness. It's alignment. Second, don't let shame preach louder than Scripture. Condemnation says you are your worst mistake. Christ says there is no condemnation for those who are in Him. Conviction leads you forward; shame chains you backward. Third, understand that marriage is daily dying, not just daily living. Love is not sustained by emotion alone. It is built on humility, patience, sacrifice, accountability, forgiveness, and steady faithfulness when no one is applauding. If you've failed before, your next chapter survives not on passion, but on surrender. Fourth, remember that God uses men with scars. Scripture is filled with imperfect people restored by grace. Your past may explain you, but it does not have the authority to define you if Christ has redeemed you.

And here's what I'd tell you straight, man to man. If you're on your third marriage like me — or if you're simply afraid, you'll ruin the one you're in — don't focus on the number. Focus on today. Guard your heart. Stay transparent when you struggle.

Inviting accountability before isolation invites temptation. Pray even when it feels awkward. Choose faithfulness, especially when it feels ordinary. God is not sitting in heaven waiting for you to slip again.

His mercies are new every morning, which means today is not chained to yesterday unless you choose to drag the chain. I don't know your whole story. I just know mine. I know what regret feels like. I know what fear of repeating patterns feels like. I know what it's like to love someone deeply and whisper, "Lord, help me not mess this up." What I've learned is this: faithfulness is not built by a perfect history. It is built by daily surrender. And maybe your story isn't ultimately about how many times you failed. Maybe it's about how deeply you learned to lean on grace.

"Sometimes the quiet thoughts of ordinary people

travel farther than we expect."

— Jim Williams

The Slow Work of Healing

Salvation felt decisive, while healing revealed itself as something far more gradual. That distinction has become one of the clearest truths I've learned along this road. Before surrender, failure pushed me away from God. Shame crept in quietly, and distance naturally followed. But after surrender, something fundamental shifted. Failure no longer sent me running from Him — it drove me toward Him. Not because I suddenly developed greater strength, but because I finally understood where grace lives. That change did not produce perfection. It produced something far more honest: a man being shaped, corrected, and refined, one uneven step at a time.

Looking back, my life no longer appears as a straight line but as a series of defining moments scattered like landmarks along a winding road. A simple invitation in a race shop. A sermon about Nicodemus. A gentle tug at my shirt. A whisper settling quietly but unmistakably: "It's time." Hard conversations that stretched my pride. Quiet obedience that humbled my will. Daily decisions that slowly carve away self-reliance. Those moments did not merely influence my story — they formed it. They became the shaping fires, the pivots, the places where God patiently redirected my course.

That reflection carried me today to Mark 2, the story of a man who could not walk and the friends who refused to let paralysis speak the final word. Jesus was teaching in a crowded house, packed wall to wall with listeners. Most people would have seen the obstacle and turned back. Too crowded. Too complicated.

Perhaps another day. But faith rarely waits for convenience.

These friends climbed the roof, tore through it, and lowered their broken companion directly into the presence of Christ. That kind of determination has a way of stopping a simple man in his tracks. How far would I go for someone else? How often do obstacles become comfortable excuses? How often do I carry faith — for others or even in myself?

What lingers most deeply is not the miracle itself but the order of Jesus' words. He does not begin with movement. He begins with restoration. "Son, your sins are forgiven." Before strength returned to limbs, freedom returned to the heart. That order matters more than we often realize. Because sometimes paralysis is not physical at all. Sometimes it is guilt, fear, regret, shame, or wounds carried quietly beneath the surface. Jesus addressed the root before the symptom.

The teachers of the law recoiled immediately, reasoning that only God could forgive sins. Yet within their objection sits one of the most profound revelations of Christ's identity. Jesus did not escalate the moment. He simply asked, "Which is easier?" Then He spoke with authority that only the divine could possess: "Get up, take your mat, and walk." And the man rose.

But what stays with me long after the scene fades is this steady pattern: forgiveness first, healing after. Salvation arrived as a moment — clear, decisive, unmistakable. Healing has unfolded as a process. Layer by layer. Lesson by lesson. Pride softened. Fear confronted. Trust rebuilt. Faith strengthened not through flashes of drama but through daily surrender. Jesus was never merely interested in symptoms. He has always been about restoration — whole restoration of heart, mind, identity, and direction.

There is another quiet truth resting within that roof-torn story. Sometimes God uses people to carry us when we cannot walk ourselves. Sometimes we are the ones being carried. Sometimes we are the ones doing the carrying. Those friends did not heal their companion. They simply refused to let obstacles prevent him from reaching Jesus. Love works like that. Prayers work like that. Faithful presence works like that. We do not fix souls — we help lower them into grace.

Healing is not always instant. Redemption rarely unfolds in a single dramatic moment. But forgiveness lays the foundation. Salvation begins the work. And Christ, steady and patient, teaches hearts how to walk again — physically, spiritually, emotionally. In this complicated world, what we may need most is not immediate solutions but restored hearts: hearts free enough to trust, strong enough to rise, and willing enough to carry others when their strength gives way.

That is the miracle still unfolding.

"Be still, and know that I am God."

— Psalm 46:10 (ESV)

The Wilderness Doesn't Come With You

When we think about the wilderness, most of us want nothing to do with it. The wilderness feels empty. It feels quiet. It feels like nothing is happening. It is a place where things slowdown in ways we don't like, where answers don't come as quickly as we want, and where we are left alone with thoughts we would rather avoid. But when you begin to look at Scripture, a pattern starts to emerge. The wilderness shows up over and over again—not just as a place of hardship, but as a place of preparation.

The wilderness is where God does some of His deepest work, not in the spotlight, but in the quiet places where it is just you and Him. Moses spent forty years in the wilderness before God ever used him to lead. The Israelites were led into the wilderness before they were allowed to step into the Promised Land, and Scripture tells us in Deuteronomy 8:2 that God used that time to humble them and test them. Elijah ran into the wilderness exhausted and afraid, only to encounter God not in power, but in a whisper. David was anointed king but spent years in the wilderness being shaped before he ever stepped into the throne. John the Baptist lived in the wilderness before his public ministry. Even Jesus was led into the wilderness before beginning His work. Paul disappeared into Arabia before stepping into his calling. The pattern is hard to ignore.

Wilderness comes before purpose. Isolation comes before impact. Preparation comes before calling is revealed. And in many of those stories, something else becomes clear—something in them had to change before they could step into what God had for them.

That is the part we do not always like to talk about. Because the wilderness is not just about where you are. It is about what God is doing in you.

That realization forced me to ask a harder question: what in me cannot go where God is taking me? Maybe it is a doubt. Maybe it is fear. Maybe it is that quiet voice that says, *you are not good enough.* Maybe it is the need for approval, or the version of myself I have been holding onto for too long. Because there are things we carry that cannot go with us into what God has prepared. Some things must be left behind.

The wilderness is where that happens. It is where God begins to strip away what does not belong so He can build what does. It is where identity is reshaped, where dependence is learned, and where trust is formed in ways it could not be anywhere else. And while it may feel like nothing is happening, it is often the place where the most important things are taking place beneath the surface.

Looking back on my own life, I see those seasons differently now. The waiting, the closed doors, the moments that did not make sense, they may not have been delays at all. They may have been preparing. And when I think about the company that comes with that, the Moses', the Davids, the Elijahs, the Paul's, even Jesus Himself, it changes how I view those seasons. It reminds me that the wilderness is not a sign that God has forgotten you. It is often a sign that He is preparing you.

From the Porch, the truth is simple: if you are in the wilderness right now, do not rush it and do not fight it. Let God do what only He can do there.

Because when you step into what He has for you, you will not take the wilderness with you—but you will carry everything God built in you because of it.

"Grace doesn't erase the wreckage—
it walks with you while you rebuild."
— Jim Williams

Thoughts of a Simple Man (…and a Somewhat Wet One)

This conversation has always been an interesting one. It's one of those porch-talk topics that can turn friendly smiles into folded arms in a hurry. Baptism. Dunking. Sprinkling. Infants. Dedications. Traditions. Denominations. I've seen good church folks get hotter over water than they ever do over fire, and if I'm honest, that alone ought to make a simple man pause.

Baptism matters. Jesus made that clear. It sits right there in the Great Commission — not as a suggestion, not as a denominational preference, but as part of the rhythm of discipleship. He didn't say, "Go and debate procedures." He said, "Go and make disciples… baptizing them." That gives the subject weight from the very beginning.

Now, when I read my Bible, some things come across pretty plain to me. Jesus went down into the water. He came up out of the water. Submerged. Not lightly sprinkled. Not symbolically misted. Wet from head to toe. Paul's words echo the imagery — burial and resurrection. Buried with Him in baptism. And burial, last I checked, isn't something accomplished with a gentle splash.

But porch conversations deserve honesty, so let's clear something up. That old story about sprinkling beginning in Russia because it was too cold. It sounds reasonable, but history tells a more layered story. Pouring or sprinkling — affusion — appears very early in Christian practice.

The Didache, one of the earliest writings outside Scripture, allowed pouring water when immersion wasn't possible. Not because of climate, but because of circumstance — lack of water, illness, persecution, practicality. Cold regions later reinforced the practice, yes, but they didn't invent it.

And that's where my simple-man brain starts turning. How did allowances for special situations slowly harden into traditions… then preferences… then dividing lines?

Infant baptism is another place where the conversation deepens. I've searched the Scriptures, and I don't see a clear example of infants being baptized. I do see children being loved, blessed, and welcomed by Jesus. I do see households mentioned — Lydia's household, the jailer's household. Some read that and conclude everyone, including infants, must have been baptized. Maybe. But I also see a consistent pattern repeated throughout Acts: they heard, they believed, they were baptized.

Belief seems to come first.

Faith, at least as I understand it, isn't inherited like a last name or eye color. At some point, the heart awakens. Awareness takes root. A person responds. Baptism then becomes the outward declaration of that inward decision — a sermon without words.

Now, I've also heard the other side, the argument that baptism isn't necessary for salvation. And there's truth worth acknowledging there. Salvation is by grace through faith. The thief on the cross didn't climb down for immersion. The water itself is not the saving agent.

But obedience still matters.

Jesus commanded baptism. The early church practiced it. Believers embraced it, not as a burden but as a testimony.

Baptism doesn't save a soul — but it certainly speaks. It declares allegiance. It symbolizes death to the old life and rising into the new.

So where do I land as a simple man in a complicated theological landscape?

For me, baptism is deeply meaningful, deeply symbolic, and — yes — best reflected through immersion. Fully wet. Fully identifying with burial and resurrection. But I've also lived long enough to recognize something else.

The water itself is rarely the real issue.

Division is.

Maybe the greater danger isn't whether someone was dunked or sprinkled. Maybe it's when we cling tighter to methods than to the mission. When we elevate procedure above unity. When we argue about water while forgetting the One baptism to which it points.

So, if someone wants to debate baptism styles, I won't fight till the porch boards creak.

But if you want to sit on the porch and talk about Jesus?

I'll grab a chair.

Jim Williams

"My grace is sufficient for you,

for my power is made perfect in weakness."

— 2 Corinthians 12:9 (ESV)

Learning to Trust When I Can't See the Map

I watched a video this week that slowed me down in the best possible way. Not because it was dramatic or emotionally charged, but because it did something far more powerful — it lingered with Scripture. It sat patiently in the places most of us rush past. My pastor has used a phrase for years that keeps echoing back to me: understand the white space. The white space is where the story breathes. The space between the verses. The details we skim because we think we already know how everything unfolds. And this video — *EXPEDITION ABRAHAM: From His Birthplace to the Promised Land* — lives right there.

Most of us know the headline version of Abraham's life. God calls. Abraham obeys. Promise given. Faith affirmed. Father of Nations. But watching the journey unfold step by step, mile by mile, river by river, made something settle deeper in me. God didn't hand Abraham a map. He didn't lay out a timeline. He didn't provide the kind of clarity we're so addicted to. He simply said, "Leave." Leave your country. Leave your people. Leave the world you understand. And go… somewhere I'll show you later.

That's the white space.

And if I'm honest, that's where I've often struggled. There have been moments in my life when I sensed God's nudge clearly. Not audible, not thunderous — but unmistakable in my spirit. "Step." "Move." "Go." Sometimes I did.

Sometimes I trusted Him enough to walk without knowing how the road would bend. And looking back now, I can see His fingerprints all over those uncertain steps. But there were other times, too. Times I stayed. Not because God was silent. Not because I didn't recognize His leading. But because fear spoke louder than faith.

I like plans. I like structure. I like knowing how things will turn out before I commit to movement. Faith rarely accommodates that preference.

Abraham didn't just leave geography — he left certainty. He walked away from Ur of the Chaldeans, a thriving city filled with infrastructure, commerce, culture, and familiarity. He walked away from everything that felt stable. I've never walked a thousand miles behind livestock, but I've sat comfortably in my own versions of "Ur." Settled. Safe. Quietly aware that obedience might require discomfort, I wasn't eager to embrace it.

He followed the Euphrates because water meant survival. He paused in Haran for a season. And I see something deeply human in that. Not rebellion — just hesitation. Half-obedience. Waiting for more explanation. Waiting for more assurance. Waiting for God to provide guarantees He never promised.

More white space.

What struck me most was not Abraham's confidence, but his trust. When he left Haran at seventy-five years old — aging, childless, carrying nothing but a word from God — faith took on an entirely different weight. Faith is not confidence in outcomes. Faith is trust in the One who calls. That distinction feels small until life presses you into a decision where clarity is absent.

I've lived long enough now to recognize something comforting in this story. The times I stepped forward, uncertain but obedient,

God met me there. The times fear anchored my feet, God remained patient. He did not abandon me for hesitating. He did not revoke His presence because my courage wavered.

By the time Abraham reached Shechem, he didn't know the terrain when he first left home. But he knew the voice that sent him.

I'm still learning to live like that. Some days obedience comes quickly. Other days, it comes with wrestling. Some days, faith feels steady. Other days fear crowds the room. But I'm beginning to understand that the white space — that stretch between "leave" and "arrival" — is where faith is either strengthened or stalled.

And maybe that's where many of us quietly live.

Maybe God has nudged you before. Toward forgiveness. Toward surrender. Toward change you couldn't fully see yet. Maybe He asked you to move without handing you the blueprint. It's uncomfortable territory. But it's also sacred ground. Abraham never saw the fullness of the promise in his lifetime. Yet he saw enough to keep walking.

That's the kind of faith I'm asking God to grow in me. Not a man who needs the entire map laid out in advance. Just a man willing to take the next step.

Because obedience still sounds the same today as it did then:

Leave… and go to the land I will show you.

And sometimes, for a simple man like me, that simply means getting up again tomorrow and choosing faith over fear — one ordinary step at a time.

"Faith isn't always loud—

sometimes it looks like showing up again tomorrow."

— Jim Williams

Learning to Trust the Voice

I was lying in bed last night, caught in that familiar kind of exhaustion where the body is ready for rest, but the mind refuses to cooperate. The room was quiet, yet my thoughts were nothing but. You just lie there staring at the ceiling, replaying fragments of the day, carrying on conversations that never happened, sorting through worries that seem louder in the dark. Somewhere in that stillness, I began talking to God the way I often do when sleep won't come. I admitted I'd missed a few days of writing — weather, sickness, distractions, excuses stacked neatly like boxes waiting to be justified. And then I asked Him the simplest question I know how to ask: "Lord, what do You want me to write about?"

And wouldn't you know it — *Days of Thunder* drifted into my mind.

I actually laughed at myself. A racecar movie from 1990 didn't exactly feel like sacred territory. But the longer I lay there, the more the thought refused to leave. There's a scene where Harry, the seasoned crew chief, is trying to guide Cole, the gifted but stubborn driver. Cole has talent — plenty of it. Speed, instinct, fearlessness. But what he lacks is trust. Everything around him has changed: the car, the track, the system, the rhythm of racing itself. Yet Cole keeps driving the only way he knows how — aggressive, relentless, pushing every lap right on the ragged edge. And in doing so, he's burning through his tires.

Harry finally offers him a challenge rooted not in criticism, but in confidence. Drive fifty laps your way, he says.

Then we'll pit, change tires, and you drive fifty laps my way. Give me an honest run — and I'll beat you every time.

That line settled deeply.

Because if I'm honest, isn't that often our story too? We say we trust God. We profess belief that He sees more than we do. Yet when life tightens, when pressure mounts, when uncertainty creeps in, our instinct is rarely to surrender. It's acceleration. Grip tighter. Push harder. Force outcomes. We run ourselves straight to exhaustion — wearing thin our patience, our peace, even our relationships — and then quietly wonder why life feels so unstable.

God doesn't look at us and say we lack ability. He doesn't dismiss our effort or condemn our instincts. Instead, He gently invites, "Try it My way." Not as an immediate lifetime overhaul. Just for a stretch. Give Him an honest run.

And then there's that other scene — the one that struck something even more personal. After Cole's devastating wreck, he lies strapped inside a CAT scan machine. Confined. Surrounded by noise. Unable to see. Unable to move. Completely out of control. And what does he ask for? Not freedom. Not explanation. Just someone to talk to him. He says he has a guy — Harry — who speaks to him over the radio.

Cole can't see him.

But he knows his voice.

And somehow, that voice steadies him.

That moment felt uncomfortably familiar. Life has a way of wrecking us at times. Not always physically, but emotionally, mentally, spiritually.

Seasons of confusion, fear, weariness, where the future feels hidden, and the noise of uncertainty echoes loudly. Moments where clarity disappears, and control slips through our fingers. And in those places, what we often need most isn't a perfectly detailed plan.

We just need to hear His voice again.

We don't see God with our eyes, yet He speaks — through Scripture, through prayer, through that quiet, persistent nudge that presses gently on the heart. A voice that doesn't shout over chaos but steadies us within it. "Easy now. Stay steady. Trust Me."

Maybe faith isn't about driving harder.

Maybe it's about trusting the One who sees the entire track — the turns hidden from view, the hazards we don't yet recognize, the wear on tires we assume are still strong. Maybe faith is loosening our grip just enough to believe His guidance is wiser than our instincts.

So maybe today, I'll ease up a little.

Maybe I'll stop living life right on the ragged edge.

Maybe I'll give God an honest run His way.

After all, He's never lost a race yet.

Jim Williams

"And we know that for those who love God

all things work together for good…"

— Romans 8:28 (ESV)

Finding Rest in God's Provision

Life moves fast. It rarely asks permission before the pace shifts. One moment things feel steady, predictable, manageable, and the next you find yourself gripping the wheel tighter than you ever intended. Pushing harder. Leaning into the turns of responsibility, expectation, and quiet pressure, trying to keep everything from sliding out of control. And if you're not careful, you begin running life right on the ragged edge, burning through emotional tires you didn't even realize were wearing thin.

After reflecting on that scene from *Days of Thunder* — the idea of trusting the calm voice over the radio rather than forcing the car through every turn — I began to recognize something uncomfortably familiar. Sometimes life feels heavier than it should. Not because life itself has changed, but because of how tightly I'm holding it. The endless to-do lists. The silent expectations. The worries that creep in when everything gets quiet. The tension that settles into the shoulders without announcement. And I can't help but wonder if, at times, I've been trying to win races I was never meant to drive alone.

Exodus 18 paints a picture that feels surprisingly modern. Moses sits from morning until evening, carrying the weight of an entire nation's disputes, questions, and decisions. He isn't rebelling. He isn't neglecting duty. He is trying to be faithful. Responsible. Obedient. And still, Jethro looks at him with simple clarity and says, in essence, "This isn't good. You're going to wear yourself out.

That truth lands with a quiet thud. Because Moses' problem wasn't disobedience — it was overloaded. Faithfulness tangled with exhaustion.

Jethro's counsel was not a corrective rooted in criticism. It was wisdom rooted in care. Share the load. Appoint leaders. Trust others with pieces of work. In other words, step out of the driver's seat occasionally. How often do I tell myself, "I can handle this"? How often do I tighten my grip when God is gently whispering, "You don't have to"?

"Cast your burden on the Lord, and He will sustain you." That word *cast* carries weight. It implies release. Transfer. Letting go of something never meant to remain clenched in human hands. And then comes Jesus' invitation, steady and unmistakably kind: "Come to Me, all who labor and are heavy laden, and I will give you rest." Do not push harder. Do not prove yourself stronger. Come. Rest. Learn.

Rest is not weakness. It is trust in motion. It is the recognition that God's provision doesn't only arrive as material blessings or visible solutions. Sometimes His provision looks like people, counsel, community, shared responsibility, or the timely wisdom of someone who sees what fatigue has blurred. Sometimes His provision is simply the reminder that I am not the Savior. He is.

Moses needed Jethro. Cole needed Harry. And I need the Lord daily to remind me when I'm trying to carry more than I was designed to hold. So today, I find myself trying again — loosening the grip, listening to the steady voice instead of the roar of pressure, humbling myself enough to accept help when it appears.

Because maybe faith isn't about driving harder. Maybe it's about knowing when to pit. When to refuel. When to rest in the provision already present. Right here. Right now. God's provision is enough. And the rest He offers was never meant to be postponed.

"The wilderness isn't where you're lost—

it's where you're being shaped."

— Jim Williams

Not on the Planning Committee, Just Watching the Sky

Resting in God's provision has taught me something else along this journey of faith: I don't have to manage the future either. I'll be honest right up front — when it comes to the rapture, I don't pretend to have it all mapped out. I've got a good friend who has studied eschatology deep — and I mean really deep. Charts, timelines, Greek word studies, and cross-references are layered like a carefully built framework. I genuinely enjoy sitting across from him with coffee in hand, listening to someone who has done the homework. Me? I sometimes feel like I'm still reading the syllabus.

I hear believers discuss pre-trib, mid-trib, and post-trib with an intensity that can rival debates about politics or sports. Opinions sharpen. Voices rise. Lines quietly form. And somewhere in the middle of those conversations, I find myself leaning back with a simpler thought: Lord, I don't need to be on the planning committee, but I'll gladly volunteer for the welcoming committee. Because while there is much I don't claim to understand, there are things Scripture makes beautifully clear.

The word rapture itself isn't printed in our English Bibles, and that alone unsettles some people. But the concept is there, drawn from a Latin term meaning "to be caught up" or "snatched away."

Paul describes that moment with a vividness that even a simple man can grasp. The Lord Himself will descend. There will be a shout, the voice of the archangel, the trumpet of God.

The dead in Christ will rise first, and those still living — still moving through ordinary days of work, responsibility, and routine — will be caught up together to meet the Lord in the air. In a flash.

In the twinkling of an eye. Not because we earned it, not because we predicted it correctly, but because of Him. That part steadies me every time I think about it. Not because I know when it happens. Not because I can diagram exactly how it aligns with tribulation. But because I know who we are meeting. Scripture calls it a mystery, something not fully revealed until God chose to unfold it. And I've come to peace with mystery. Life itself has taught me that God does not owe me a detailed itinerary of His plans. He is God. I am not. That arrangement has never failed Him, and it has served me well to accept it.

Some believe the rapture is distinct from the second coming, separate events with separate purposes. Others see it as one unfolding reality viewed from different angles. Some say believers will be spared from tribulation altogether. Others believe we may walk straight through hardship before Christ gathers His people. I listen. I learn. I consider. But ultimately, I rest here: if God calls His people to endure tribulation, then so be it. If He calls us home before it, then glory to God. Either way, He holds the plan, and I do not have to carry the burden of managing what only He controls.

Paul did not write about these things to fracture the church. He wrote to comfort it. To encourage believers living under pressure, persecution, and uncertainty. "Encourage one another with these words." That is the heart of it. Not arguments.

Not speculation. Encouragement. Hope. Assurance that this broken world is not our permanent address.

What I know is simple and sufficient. One day, these weary bones will change. One day, faith will give way to sight. One day, the voice we've trusted without seeing will stand before us in full clarity.

Whether I rise from the ground or am caught up from the air, I will be with the Lord forever. That is enough for a simple man.

So, I will keep listening. I will keep learning. But I won't spend my days fighting over seating charts in heaven. I'll keep my eyes lifted, my heart ready, and my name written down for the welcoming committee — not the planning committee. Just watching the sky.

Jim Williams

"Come to me, all who labor and are heavy laden,

and I will give you rest."

— Matthew 11:28 (ESV)

The Brother Who Saw Me

Sometimes the moments that shape us most are not the loud, dramatic ones that everyone notices. Sometimes they arrive quietly, almost gently, through something as simple and as powerful as being truly seen by another person. Not observed. Not evaluated. But seen. For me, that moment came through my brother, Sammy.

He was not the brother I grew up alongside every day. We did not share the same household, the same routines, the same early memories. He lived with my dad, my stepmom, and our half-brothers, while my life unfolded along a different road entirely. We shared the same father and the same blood, yet our worlds were written in separate chapters. He did not know the full story of why I was not there, the circumstances and choices that shaped the distance between us. And if I am honest, I did not fully understand his world either. We were connected by family yet separated by experience.

But life has a way of surprising us. There came a time when Sammy entered my life not simply as a distant sibling, but as a man seeing another man. Something shifted in that space. There were no lectures, no attempts to fix or rewrite the past, no reminders of what could have been different. He did something far more meaningful. He noticed me. He saw my struggles without magnifying them. He saw my efforts without measuring them against perfection. He saw the person I was becoming rather than the history we did not share. And in that quiet recognition, something inside me steadied.

There is a kind of healing that does not come through advice or correction. It comes through acknowledgment. Through the simple gift of someone saying, without words, "I see you, and I am here." That kind of seeing changes a person. It reminds you that even if life did not begin side by side, walking together from this point forward is still possible. It reminds you that connection is not limited to childhood, that relationships can grow later, that grace can step into spaces long marked by absence or misunderstanding.

I know many people understand that kind of story. Families are rarely as tidy as we imagine they should be. There are gaps, distances, misunderstandings, and years that do not line up the way we hoped. Yet there remains the possibility of something new. Of being seen. Moving toward understanding. Of grace entering where history left rough edges. We are all, in one way or another, messy people navigating imperfect stories.

What Sammy gave me was not instructions. It was recognition. And recognition carries a quiet power that correction alone often cannot. It affirms dignity. It restores connection. It reminds us that we are more than the sum of our circumstances. When someone sees that truth and chooses to walk beside you anyway, it becomes one of life's defining gifts.

I have tried to carry that lesson forward. To notice people more carefully. To acknowledge effort even when outcomes are imperfect. To recognize the person behind the struggle. Because sometimes what truly changes a life is not being corrected. It is being seen.

The brother I did not grow up with but later walked beside me taught me something simple and lasting: people matter deeply. And often, the people God places in our lives become His quiet way of showing up — steadying, guiding, reminding us that even delayed bonds can become defining ones. Some stories do not unfold in straight lines. Some relationships do not begin the way we expect. But grace has a way of meeting us, anyway, weaving connection where distance once lived.

And for that, I remain grateful.

"God wastes nothing—

not the years, not the failures,

not even the things we wish we could undo."

— Jim Williams

Respect for the Walk

L et me tell you about something that stirred up more conversation than I expected. A group of venerable monks recently walked through our town, part of a journey that stretched two thousand three hundred miles on foot from Fort Worth to Washington, D.C. They called it a walk for peace, and I'll admit, it stirred something in me — a mixture of admiration and unease. The admiration came first. Discipline alone commands respect. Walking that distance, surrendering comfort, enduring exhaustion, weather, aching muscles, blistered feet — all for the sake of conviction. In a world built on convenience, where discomfort is often treated like an emergency, that kind of commitment deserves an honest pause. But respect for dedication does not require agreement with doctrine. You can honor effort without embracing the message behind it.

At the heart of their journey lies a belief that peace is something cultivated from within, something uncovered through discipline, meditation, and the quieting of the self. That is not the peace Jesus described. Scripture does not present peace as a human achievement or a mental state we manufacture through effort. It presents peace as a gift. "Peace, I leave with you; My peace I give to you. Not as the world gives do I give to you." That distinction is not small. The world often teaches that peace rises from inside us. Jesus teaches that peace flows from Him. One centers on self-attainment. The other on divine grace. And when Christians urge discernment, it is not fear speaking, nor mockery, nor insecurity. It is love — the same kind of love that warns when a bridge ahead is out.

But caution is not condemnation. Hospitality is not a compromise. These men are image-bearers of God, worthy of kindness, dignity, and respect. One can offer water, shake hands, teach children gentleness, and remain anchored in conviction. Jesus Himself held compassion and truth together without tension. He loved deeply without affirming error. He showed grace without surrendering holiness. That balance remains necessary today, especially in a time when spiritual messages often sound gentle, warm, and reasonable while quietly drifting from the center of Christ. Truth remains truth, whether it arrives wrapped in comfort or discomfort. Scripture, all of it, still stands God-breathed and steady.

Every walk points somewhere. Every message carries a destination. Discernment is not hostility; it is faithfulness. We are called to love people sincerely while measuring ideas carefully. Kindness and clarity are not enemies. They belong together. A simple man does not need to win arguments or raise his voice above the noise. He simply needs to remain faithful — respectful toward people, discerning toward messages, anchored in truth.

And that brings me to another porch-sitter of a thought — the matter of hearing God in a noisy world. I believe God speaks, not because it sounds dramatic or mystical, but because a relationship requires communication. God is not interested in distance. He is not confined to ancient pages alone. Yet I've never heard Him in an audible voice. No thunder, no booming echo, no spectacle. But He has spoken to my heart in ways that carried a clarity too steady to ignore. Promptings that unsettled sleep. Warnings I didn't fully grasp at the time. Confirmations that later surfaced through Scripture, through circumstances, through voices I hadn't influenced. That confirmation matters because God does not stir confusion for drama's sake. He confirms what He impresses.

I've had moments I still struggle to fully explain — impressions that later proved painfully accurate, insights that only made sense in hindsight. But experience itself is never the anchor. Scripture is.

God speaks most clearly through what He has already said. The Bible remains the steady voice against which every thought must be measured. God does not contradict Himself. He does not rush toward sin. His voice, even when convicting, carries a strange peace — not chaos, not pressure, not panic. The enemy pushes. Fear shouts. Ego demands. God invites.

Over time, His tone becomes familiar. Not always comfortable, but steady. And humility becomes essential. The wisest posture is rarely "God told me." It is often "I believe God may be leading — what do you see?" Because God values obedience more than information, and wisdom more than spectacle. The Spirit does not invent new truth; He illuminates eternal truth. He brings Scripture to mind. He unsettles drift. He steadies fear. He never leads where Christ would not walk.

For those who feel God is silent, I offer this gentle encouragement: He is not far. He is not withholding. The noise is often louder than His whisper. Pull up a chair. Open His Word. Quiet the distractions. Listen — not for thunder, but for truth. The porch is a good place for that.

Jim Williams

"The steps of a man are established by the Lord…"

— Psalm 37:23 (ESV)

When the Flames Reveal Grace

I remember that day with the clarity that time has never managed to dull, even though it sits decades behind me now. I was a firefighter then, and I loved every heartbeat of that life — the sirens tearing through the air, the crackle of radios, the smell of smoke and heat that followed me home like a second skin. Chaos felt familiar. It felt purposeful. Leaving that world later would become one of the hardest transitions of my life. There are moments I still wonder about it, moments when memory pulls at me. But then I steady myself with a simple truth: had I stayed, I wouldn't be the man I am now.

That afternoon began as nothing remarkable. My first wife was home cooking chicken for dinner. I ran to the store for something small, my mind occupied with ordinary thoughts — groceries, supper, routine. Nothing dramatic. Nothing urgent. Just life moves along like it always does. And then, out of nowhere, the engine's dispatch crackled across the scanner. My address. My house. On fire. In an instant, the world tilted. The stomach drops before the mind catches up. The body moves before logic and has time to argue. By the time I arrived, smoke was already pushing through the curtains, flames licking along the walls, my heart pounding in a rhythm only adrenaline understands.

She was fine. Thank God, she was fine. That remains the part I return to first. The house itself had taken the hit, but life — precious, irreplaceable life — stood untouched. But what unfolded next is what truly etched that day into my soul.

Before the hot spots were even fully extinguished, before the scene had settled into its exhausted stillness, the fire department families began to appear. Not with pity. Not with spectacle. Not whispered worry. But with hands ready to help. One family, without hesitation, opened the doors of their summer cottage on the river and told us to stay there while our home was repaired. No contracts. No conditions. No expectations. Just generosity flowing as naturally as breath.

That was love in motion. "Carry each other's burdens, and in this way, you will fulfill the law of Christ." I didn't just read that verse that day — I watched it breathe. I saw devotion without self-interest, kindness without calculation. "Be devoted to one another in love. Honor one another above yourselves." It was a glimpse of what the church is meant to be at its best: not polished, not impressive, but faithful, present, and willing to show up when life fractures without warning.

Looking back, I've come to see something else in that fire. Sometimes flames are not only instruments of destruction. Sometimes they are instruments of revelation. I don't mourn the chicken, the curtains, or even the house itself. What I carry forward is the grace the moment revealed — the goodness of people, the strength of community, the quiet, steady ways God often shows up through human hands.

And in the middle of that chaos, in the smoke and confusion and unexpected loss, I saw something deeply familiar. The shape of steady faith. Small. Present. Unwavering. The kind Sammy lived. The kind God extends to us every single day. Sometimes it takes heat to notice it. Sometimes grace becomes most visible in the moments that feel like they're burning everything down.

Why Fire So Often Follows the Furnace

I've heard it said more times than I can count that revival always comes through persecution. When you look at history, it's easy to see why people say that. The church gets squeezed, scattered, or pushed into corners, and suddenly faith seems to ignite with fresh intensity. But sitting quietly with Jesus' words, "Blessed are those who hunger and thirst for righteousness," I find myself asking a simpler, quieter question: why does it so often take hardship to wake us up? And maybe an even more uncomfortable one follows close behind — if our hearts stayed hungry, if our spiritual ovens stayed warm, would persecution even be necessary to stir revival at all?

Persecution has a way of stripping life down to essentials. Comfort fades. Distractions lose their grip. The illusions we build around stability and self-sufficiency begin to crumble. When faith starts costing something, we stop treating it like an accessory and start clinging to God like oxygen. Acts paint that picture vividly. When persecution scattered the believers from Jerusalem, Scripture says those who were scattered went about preaching the word. They did not retreat into silence. They did not shrink back into fear. Pressure did not extinguish their faith — it revealed it. The fire was already there. Persecution simply burned away what was unnecessary.

Peter echoes that same truth when he writes about trials testing the genuineness of faith. Fire proves what is real. Hardship exposes the difference between inherited belief and living trust.

But here is where the simple man in me keeps landing: persecution itself is not the source of revival. The Bible never says suffering is what carries power. It says God's presence does. Revival follows persecution, not because pain is holy, but because pain often removes the comforts that kept us from depending fully on Him.

Long before persecution intensified, the early church was already thriving. They were devoted to teaching, fellowship, prayer, and the shared life of faith. And the Lord added to their number daily. That was a presence culture before persecution culture. Their fire was not sparked by crisis; it was sustained by closeness to God. So, when hardship came, the flame spread rather than flickering. Pressure revealed what devotion had already been built.

I think about Sammy when I reflect on this. Life was not always easy for him, yet his heart carried a steadiness that did not depend on crisis. There is something powerful about quiet, persistent devotion. About keeping the ovens warm on ordinary days. About tending the fire when life feels calm rather than waiting for storms to force us back to hunger. Cold ovens create the need for crisis. But warm ovens sustain life long before hardship arrives.

Sometimes persecution accomplishes what comfort would not. It drives us back to the essentials. Back to prayer. Back to dependence. Back to hunger. Not because God has left us, but because we have drifted into forgetfulness. Hebrews reminds us that the Lord disciplines those He loves. Discipline is not rejected. It is correct. It is God refusing to let His people live indefinitely on cold bread and fading fire.

But here is the hope that steadies me: if we remain hungry, we do not have to wait for persecution to awaken us. If we abide in Christ daily, revival ceases to be a reaction and becomes a residence.

Jesus did not describe abiding as an occasional return. He described it as a way of living. A steady nearness. Continuous dependence.

Paul captured that same rhythm when he spoke of rejoicing always and praying without ceasing. That is not revival as an event. That is presence as a lifestyle. Maybe revival often follows persecution because hardship restores hunger. But perhaps God's greater desire is that we never lose that hunger in the first place. I do not want suffering to be the thing that reminds me I need God. I want warm ovens on ordinary mornings. Fresh bread when life feels unremarkable. A faith that burns steadily, not only bright.

Because in a complicated world, the simplest revival may not be dramatic at all. It may simply be this: staying hungry, staying near, and living every day as though God's presence is already enough — because it is.

"I didn't need a new life plan—

I needed a new direction."

— Jim Williams

Wrestling with Temptation and Trust

Some days, the weight of temptation presses down like a storm cloud you can't quite outrun. Some days, the pull of this world feels relentless, tugging at the mind, the heart, the will, until you're left wondering which way is steady and which way is shifting sand. Lately, I've found myself sitting quietly more often, trying to listen, trying to breathe, trying to sort through the noise that life so easily piles on. Because if I'm honest, the walk of faith isn't always loud victories and mountaintop clarity. Sometimes it's simply standing still when everything inside you feels unsettled.

God's love is vast beyond comprehension, yet disarmingly simple in its invitation. It was never about performing well enough, achieving moral perfection, or earning some invisible approval. It's about knowing Him. Trusting Him. Walking with Him. And yet, knowing Him can feel harder than we expect. Fear creeps in. Doubt whispers. That old familiar voice reminds us of every failure, every weakness, every place we feel we've fallen short. "You're not enough," it says. And maybe that's where grace quietly answers, "You never were meant to be on your own."

Paul spoke of a thorn in the flesh, something persistent, something humbling, something that kept him leaning on God rather than himself. I've wondered if our struggles often serve the same purpose. Not as punishment, but as refinement. Not as evidence of God's distance, but as reminders of our dependence. Weaknesses have a way of teaching trust that strength never could. It strips away illusions of self-sufficiency.

It drives us back to prayer, back to surrender, back to the quiet realization that His power is made perfect not in our control, but in our need.

I'm learning something that feels both small and heavy at the same time: it's okay not to have everything figured out. Faith was never built on complete understanding. Maybe each morning is simply a choice — to lay down the worries that waited for us overnight, to loosen our grip on doubt, to trust His loved one more day. One breath. One step. One quiet act of surrender at a time.

And here I am, still just a simple man walking through a complicated world. Leaning on the One who is never unstable, never uncertain, never overwhelmed by the storms that rattle me. And remembering Sammy — his quiet steadiness, his unspoken trust, the way his life reminded me that grace is larger than fear, stronger than failure, and always present even when the road feels unclear. Some lessons aren't taught through sermons. Some are living. And some stay with you long after the voice that carried them has gone quiet.

Let's Talk About Crab Grass

L et's talk about crabgrass. Yes… crabgrass—that annoying weed we all find creeping into our yards. The kind that spreads quietly, takes root where you don't notice, and before long… starts taking over. If you don't deal with it, it will choke out everything else.

After I was saved—after my time on the mountain at Quest, I began asking questions. Hard questions. Where did my struggles start? Where did they take root? I wanted answers. I wanted freedom. I wanted to beat those struggles with everything I had. I wanted to grab them, pull them up by the root, and destroy them once and for all. So, I searched… and I searched… and I prayed, "Lord, show me where this started. Show me the root."

And one day, God gave me a word. Crabgrass. I remember thinking the same thing you probably are right now, crabgrass? But then He began to show me something. Crabgrass doesn't grow like other weeds. It spreads low, along the ground, moving quietly, dropping new roots as it goes. By the time you notice it, it's already connected in places you didn't even realize. And when you try to pull it up, you don't just pull one root; you end up chasing it across the yard.

That's when God spoke clearly: "Stop focusing on the crab grass." Because if all you do is chase it, you'll spend your whole life running from root to root, sin to sin, struggle to struggle, never feeling like you've actually won.

Instead, He said, "Focus on your yard." Groom it. Feed it. Water it. Because a healthy yard will do what your hands cannot, it will choke out the crabgrass.

And at that moment, everything shifted. Instead of chasing down every struggle and trying to trace it back to its origin, I began to focus on Jesus. Not the problem, but the Savior. Scripture says, "Fixing our eyes on Jesus, the author and perfecter of our faith…"

And when we keep looking around, at our struggles, our past, our failures, we lose direction. But when we keep our eyes on Him, something begins to change.

We begin to grow. We begin to strengthen. We begin to become something healthier. And just like that yard, the things that once had a hold on us begin to lose their grip—not because we chased them down, but because we outgrew them.

Jesus said, "Abide in Me, and I in you… He who abides in Me bears much fruit." That's the key. Abide. Stay connected. Keep tending to what God is growing in you. Now I'm not saying the struggle disappears overnight, it doesn't. But I can tell you this, it gets easier. Not because you got stronger, but because your roots went deeper in the right place.

This walk is daily. It's intentional. It's growth over time. And the more you focus on Him, the less power the crab grass has. So maybe today, instead of asking, "Where did this come from?" ask, "Am I tending my yard?"

Focus on your yard.

75

"For I know the plans I have for you…"

— Jeremiah 29:11 (ESV)

Hope Through Tribulation

As a simple man navigating a complicated world, I often find myself overwhelmed by the noise, the uncertainty, and the weight of everyday life. Some days, the pressures feel relentless, as though the world itself is pressing in from every side. In moments like that, my heart has learned where to turn. I find myself drawn back to Scripture, to those steady truths that do not shift with headlines or circumstances. Romans 5 is one of those places I return to again and again, because it speaks with such clarity about the reality of our brokenness, the depth of God's grace, and the unshakable hope we have in Jesus Christ.

Paul writes, "Therefore, just as sin entered the world through one man, and death through sin, and in this way, death came to all people, because all sinned." That single verse captures something we feel every day, whether we can articulate it or not. There is a fracture running through the human story. Through Adam's disobedience, sin entered the world, and with it came separation, struggle, and death. Every one of us lives under the shadow of that inherited brokenness. We see it in the world. We see it in others. If we are honest, we see it in ourselves. And at times, that reality can feel heavy.

But Romans 5 does not leave us staring only at the weight of sin. It quickly moves our eyes to something far greater. "But God demonstrates His own love for us in this: While we were still sinners, Christ died for us." There is something deeply humbling about that truth.

God did not wait for humanity to repair what it had broken. He did not stand at a distance demanding improvement. He stepped directly into the mess. Christ's death was not a reward for righteousness; it was a rescue for the undeserving. That is grace in its purest form — unearned, relentless, and anchored entirely in the love of God, and that grace brings more than forgiveness.

Paul tells us that being justified through faith gives us peace with God. Peace — not as a passing emotion, but as a restored relationship. Through Jesus Christ, we have access to the grace in which we now stand, and we are invited to live in the hope of the glory of God. That hope is not fragile optimism. It is a steady assurance that God's work is ongoing, even when life feels uncertain, even when circumstances feel chaotic.

What has always struck me is that Paul does not pretend suffering disappears in the Christian life. Instead, he reframes it. "We also glory in our sufferings, because we know that suffering produces perseverance; perseverance, character; and character, hope." The trials we wish away often become the very tools God uses to shape us. Hardship stretches us. It refines us. It exposes what is temporary and strengthens what is eternal. Hope is not born in comfort. It is forged in endurance.

I have seen this not only in my own life but in the lives of those who have walked beside me. Sammy comes to mind. He embodied this truth not through speeches or grand declarations, but through steady presence, quiet faith, and patient endurance. Watching someone live with that kind of grounded hope makes Scripture feel less like ink on a page and more like something alive. Our struggles, painful as they may be, can become the soil in which God grows perseverance, character, and ultimately, hope.

And this is where Romans 5 lands with such quiet power: "Hope does not put us to shame, because God's love has been poured out into our hearts through the Holy Spirit." That is the anchor. Not my strength. Not my ability to endure. His love is actively present within us. The Spirit does not merely comfort from a distance; He fills, sustains, and steadies the heart.

As a simple man, I still wrestle with the complexities of life. I still have days when the weight feels heavy. But Romans 5 reminds me why I keep looking up. Sin may be real. Suffering may be real. But grace is greater. And hope — rooted in the love of God — is never misplaced.

"Sometimes obedience is the only thing that makes sense

when nothing else does."

— Jim Williams

Walking Through Shadows with Love

Sammy and I, at the campground, — one of those quiet days that mattered more than any grand moment.

It is often in the quiet moments of life that memories rise most clearly. Today was one of those days. My mind drifted back to the time when my brother, Sammy, was still here, when his laughter filled the air like sunlight pouring through an open window. We were just two ordinary men, born into a world that has never been simple, carrying burdens that often felt heavier than the joys we celebrated. Yet in the middle of all of it, we had each other. There was a bond between us that stood steady even when life itself did not. Sammy was four years younger than me, and like most people, I had always assumed life would follow the order we expect — that the older would go before the younger. I imagined that if I ever stood behind a pulpit for a funeral, it would be for my father first. That simply felt like the natural sequence of things. But life does not always follow the order we assume.

I had officiated at many weddings before. I had stood smiling, watching couples make promises about forever.

I had prayed blessings over beginnings, over hope, over life stretching forward. But this was different. This was my first funeral, and it was my brother's. The morning the news came, it felt as though the ground had shifted beneath me. Colors dulled. Sounds faded. The world seemed to narrow into something smaller and heavier. I remember sitting in stillness, staring at a wall, trying to gather pieces of a heart that suddenly felt hollowed out. It is a strange thing to preach hope when your own heart is breaking, to speak words of comfort when your own spirit feels undone.

In that fragile emptiness, I wrestled deeply with God's sovereignty. How could a loving God allow such pain? Questions without neat answers circled endlessly through my thoughts. I remembered Sammy's gentle spirit — the kindness and softness in him that touched everyone he met — and I struggled to understand why his light seemed to dim so early. Grief, in its first moments, does not concern itself with theology. It simply hurts. I knew the verses. I knew the promises of heaven, reunion, and glory. But knowing something and feeling something are not the same. Grief has a way of exposing that gap with painful clarity.

Even now, there are days when sorrow rolls over me unexpectedly. I'll hear a joke and instinctively think, "I need to tell Sammy." I'll see something that would have made him laugh and reach for my phone before reality settles back in. That remembering stings every time. Yet even within the ache, love remains. The love I carry for my brother is a testament to what we shared. Death does not erase that bond. If anything, it magnifies how sacred our time together truly was. Standing there to preach at his funeral changed me. It forced me to live what I claim to believe. It pushed me to lean not on explanations, but on trust.

Psalm 34:18 says, "The Lord is close to the brokenhearted and saves those who are crushed in spirit."

I clung to that promise, not because I felt strong, but because I felt crushed. Somewhere in the middle of tears and trembling words, I realized something both simple and profound: walking through shadows with love means you keep loving even when it hurts.

You honor the memory. You carry the lessons forward. You speak their name with gratitude, not only grief. Sammy, I miss you still — your laughter, your gentle heart, the way you saw people. Thank you for being my brother, my companion, my reminder that love does not have to be loud to be powerful. This was my first funeral, not the one I expected or felt prepared for, but even in the shadow of death, love stood firm. And somehow, by God's grace, it still does.

"For we walk by faith, not by sight."

— 2 Corinthians 5:7 (ESV)

When Peace Sounds Right but Costs Too Much

Let me say this before I even begin. I know this won't be popular, but truth rarely is. The disciples didn't lose their lives for preaching generic kindness or promoting vague spirituality. They were persecuted and killed for proclaiming one thing with unmistakable clarity: Jesus is the only way. So, I'm not surprised when conversations like this feel uncomfortable. We live in a world where peace is often treated as the highest value — as long as it doesn't require repentance, surrender, or the acknowledgment that one path may be true while another is not.

I've seen many comments lately suggesting that Buddhism isn't a religion, and I find myself respectfully disagreeing. By any honest definition, Buddhism is indeed a religion. It contains spiritual teachings, moral frameworks, sacred texts, rituals, and a defined understanding of human purpose and destiny. It may differ greatly from Christianity, particularly in its view of God, but it is still a spiritual system with beliefs about life, suffering, and ultimate peace. And that distinction matters, because not all spiritual paths lead to Christ.

Now, let me be clear about something important. I do not support hateful speech, mocking, or hostility toward anyone. That behavior does not reflect Jesus. Christ did not insult people into repentance. We are called to love, to show respect, and to walk humbly. But love is not the same as spiritual agreement.

There is a difference between honoring someone's humanity and participating in their message.

What concerns me is not kindness toward others, but moments where believers blur theological lines, bowing, receiving spiritual blessings, or engaging in religious expressions that do not point to Jesus Christ. Scripture speaks plainly: "You shall worship the Lord your God, and Him only shall you serve." That word *only* carries weight.

Jesus welcomed sinners, yet He never affirmed sin. He forgave, but He also called for transformation. He didn't say, "Follow Me and keep everything else too." He said, "Repent." He spoke of surrender, of taking up one's cross. That is not hatred; it is holiness. Buddhism teaches that peace is found through inward discipline, meditation, detachment, and self-enlightenment. Christianity teaches that peace is found through repentance, surrender, and the finished work of Christ. Buddhism offers self-awakening. Jesus offers new birth. Buddhism does not present a Savior. Christianity stands entirely upon One. "There is salvation in no one else." That statement is not arrogance — it is conviction.

It's important to say this plainly as well: Buddhists are not evil people. Many are thoughtful, disciplined, kind, and sincere. But sincerity and truth are not identical. And when eternity is part of the conversation, distinctions matter. The world around us is anxious, divided, and exhausted. Peace sounds appealing, even necessary. But a simple man must still ask: what does that peace cost? Does it cost repentance? Does it cost truth? Does it cost Christ? Scripture warns that deception does not always appear harsh or monstrous. Often it appears reasonable, compassionate, and calming. "For when they say, 'Peace and safety,' then sudden destruction comes." Deception rarely screams. It whispers. And whispers can feel comforting in a noisy world.

So where does that leave us? Love people deeply. Respect their dignity. Offer kindness without compromise. Stand firm without becoming harsh. Live with compassion without surrendering clarity.

Because peace that flows from Christ does not require us to diminish truth. The only peace that doesn't ultimately cost too much is the peace that has already been paid for at the cross.

"Faith isn't knowing the path—

it's trusting the One who does."

— Jim Williams

When Nations Rage and Hearts Tremble

Watching the sky is one thing. Standing on the ground is another. If I'm honest, it's often easier to talk about heaven than it is to deal with headlines. It is easier to think about the trumpet than the turmoil. But if we are still here, we are still breathing, still walking, still calling us, we don't get to float above the struggle. We stand in it. And when I watch the world, it's easy to feel small. Evil can seem loud, bold, and organized, with systems moving and people plotting. Psalm 2 captures that picture with unsettling clarity: "The nations rage, and the peoples plot in vain." You can almost hear the noise inside those words.

There is no denying that unity carries power. Organized unbelief moves together with shared purpose, rallying, strategizing, pressing forward with determination. Believers, by contrast, too often scatter, argue, or divide over secondary matters. We sometimes wait for someone else to step up — someone louder, braver, or more influential. Yet Scripture reminds us that unity itself is not a danger. Babel was scattered not because unity existed, but because unity moved apart from God. Unity detached from Him is dangerous; unity under His authority is powerful. And we already know the ending. Revelation makes it unmistakably clear that Christ triumphs. Evil does not get the final word. But knowing the ending never meant folding our hands while the present unfolds.

God does not call His people to watch the world from a distance. He calls us to stand faithfully within it — to speak, to act, to remain steady. Jesus Himself modeled that balance perfectly.

He turned the other cheek. He prayed for His enemies. He wept over brokenness. He also overturned tables, confronted corruption, and spoke truth with authority. Perfect love does not eliminate righteous action; it guides it. And that tension still confronts us today. If Jesus walked our streets now, would He ignore deception? Would He remain silent where truth was being distorted? Even knowing the outcome, He acted. Always.

We live in a time when unbelief can appear relentless, narratives are carefully shaped, conviction is often misunderstood, and faith is sometimes sidelined. The temptation toward passivity is real. However, this is also a reminder that we are called to be salt and light. Salt preserves. Light exposes. Neither fulfills its purpose by accident. Yet here is where a simple man must tread carefully. We are not called to fight like the world fights. Our weapons are not hatred, bitterness, or anger disguised as righteousness. Paul reminds us that our battle is not against flesh and blood. That truth reshapes the tone entirely. We do not attack people; we confront lies. We do not despise image-bearers; we resist deception.

Ecclesiastes tells us there is a season for everything — a time to be silent and a time to speak, a time for peace and a time for war. Wisdom is knowing which season we are in. This is not a season for cowardice, but neither is it a season for cruelty. God calls His people to live as peacemakers and warriors at the same time — to stand firm without becoming hardened, to speak boldly without losing tenderness, to act courageously without surrendering compassion.

What steadies me in all of this is simple and unchanging: the world may be unstable, the battle may be real, but God remains sovereign, and the victory remains secure. Watching the sky reminds me of where this story ends. Standing on the ground reminds me why I am still here.

So, I will keep my eyes lifted and my feet planted, ready to wait when He says wait, ready to move when He says move, trusting that even when the nations rage, the King still reigns.

"Cast all your anxieties on him…"

— 1 Peter 5:7 (ESV)

Remembering More Than the Day

Standing firm in a raging world requires something else too: memory. Not merely the memory of headlines or anniversaries, but the deeper remembering of who we are and whose we are. Hmmm… have we forgotten? It had been twenty-four years since that clear September morning when everything seemed to stop. The sky was blue; the air was still and then smoke cut across it like a wound. The Twin Towers fell. The Pentagon burned. A quiet field in Pennsylvania became sacred ground. For a brief moment, we felt like one nation under God in a way that carried unusual weight. Churches filled. Flags waved. Strangers embraced. Leaders stood shoulder to shoulder. We said with conviction, "We will never forget." But time has a way of softening even the sharpest edges. Grief slowly blends into routine. Promises drift into preference. What once felt sacred becomes political. And now, years later, I find myself quietly asking: have we?

As a simple man, I try to hold that question carefully. Because one thing I refuse to do is judge hearts — only God sees those. Yet I do wrestle with what it means for a nation that once cried out to Him in unison. Are we growing stronger, or simply growing more comfortable in a world that increasingly pushes Him toward the margins? Scripture steadies me when those thoughts begin to spiral. Romans reminds us that there is no authority except that which God allows. Daniel tells us God removes kings and sets up kings.

Those verses don't say I must like every leader or agree with every direction. They remind me that heaven's throne has never been unsettled by earthly elections.

God is not surprised by shifting governments, changing cultures, or rotating leaders. Sometimes authority comes as a blessing, sometimes as testing, sometimes as discipline, sometimes as refinement. But never as chaos beyond His control.

And then there is that whisper repeated throughout Scripture: "Fear not, for I am with you." Moses heard it. Joshua heard it. Israel heard it. And we still need to hear it. No matter who holds office. No matter which party rises or falls. Fear has never been the language of faith. Jesus Himself established order when He said to give to Caesar what belongs to Caesar and to God what belongs to God. Governments will always shift. Nations will always move through seasons of unrest. But the believer's ultimate allegiance has never belonged to ballots, buildings, or banners. Our hope was never meant to rest there.

I will always remember 9/11 — the heroes who ran toward smoke, the passengers who stood against evil, the families who still carry quiet grief, the prayers that rose from broken ground. But perhaps the most important thing to remember is not only the tragedy itself, but what it awakened in us: dependence, humility, and the sobering awareness that life is fragile while God is not. "Never forget" cannot simply mean recalling the event; it must also mean remembering our need. Because city halls may change, governors may change, presidents may change, cultures may drift, and nations may rage — but God remains. Heaven's throne never trembles. And if He truly holds the world, then even in the noise, even in the uncertainty, we have nothing to fear. Hmmm… maybe that is what remembering really means.

Caring, Curiosity, and the Heart of Faith

I f we're going to stand firm when the world rages and if we're going to hold tightly to what truly matters, then we also have to learn how to love people who don't believe as we do. Courage without compassion has a way of turning hard, and conviction without love can become brittle. So let me pull a chair up close for this one. This isn't about culture wars or shouting matches. This is about coffee tables, break rooms, Scout stores — real conversations with real people who have real names and real stories.

I have friends at work who are Jehovah's Witnesses. Good people. Hardworking, kind, devoted to what they believe. We respect each other, and if one of them ever needed help, I wouldn't hesitate to show up. That's simply what love does. But if I'm honest, there are moments when I feel something deeper too — not frustration, not judgment, but a quiet kind of sorrow. Jesus said, "Blessed are those who mourn, for they shall be comforted," and sometimes mourning isn't only about loss in the physical sense. Sometimes it's about the ache you feel when someone you genuinely care about may not see Jesus the way you do. That sorrow doesn't rise from superiority; it rises from love.

Jehovah's Witnesses hold convictions about Scripture and the nature of Christ that differ from historic Christian doctrine, particularly in their understanding of Jesus. From where I stand, I hold firmly to the belief that Christ is fully God and fully man — not created, not lesser, but God in the flesh. Yet loving my friends doesn't mean I shout doctrine across a lunch table.

It means I speak gently, clearly, and with patience when the door for conversation opens. Loving someone never requires pretending we agree. It requires caring enough to hold truth without weaponizing it.

I've also had Mormon friends, some of whom I met through Scouts. I remember simple, easy conversations filled with curiosity and laughter rather than tension. That experience taught me something valuable: friendship does not require theological agreement — it requires respect. Mormons speak openly about God, Jesus, and the Holy Spirit, yet their understanding differs from traditional Christian teaching. They do not affirm the historic doctrine of the Trinity, and they embrace additional texts as scripture. From my Christian perspective, I believe Scripture is complete and that the Bible stands as God's final written revelation. That conviction is not spoken with anger but with clarity. Sincerity is real. Devotion is real. But sincerity and truth are not always identical. So how do we live inside that tension? Perhaps the way Jesus often did. He asked questions. He listened. He invited people into thought rather than forcing them into arguments. Curiosity does not equal compromise. I can listen without surrendering conviction. I can value someone without affirming every belief they hold.

At the center of it all is love — not sentimental love or blind agreement, but biblical love. Love that serves. Love that listens. Love that speaks truth with gentleness. Love that refuses to reduce human beings to labels. If we truly believe truth matters, then how we carry that truth matters just as much.

Paul wrote about "speaking the truth in love," and those two elements were never meant to be separated. Friendship requires humility. Spiritual concern requires compassion.

Mourning for someone spiritually is not looking down on them; it is caring deeply enough to desire what you believe is life-giving and eternal.

And here is something I continue learning, sometimes slowly: I don't have to argue with anyone into the Kingdom. I don't have to win debates or prove myself clever.

My calling is simpler, though not always easier. Live faithfully. Serve consistently. Love sincerely. Speak clearly when the opportunity arises. God does the saving. I do the loving. And if Jesus were sitting at my table, the question I hope I could answer with peace is this: would He recognize my tone as His? Because in a world full of noise, shifting culture, and endless division, what may speak loudest is not my argument — but my heart.

"Worry talks loud—

but truth stands steady."

— Jim Williams

Freedom and Faith

Come on up here on the porch for a minute. This one's been rattling around in my head like loose change in a mason jar. I love Jesus — not in a cultural way, not in a nostalgic way, not simply because I grew up around church — but genuinely, deeply love Him. And I do believe this country was shaped by principles that echo Scripture: human dignity, moral law, accountability before a higher authority, and freedom of conscience. The fingerprints are there if you look close enough. But here's the tension that keeps nudging at my thoughts. This nation did not establish Christianity as the national religion. It established freedom. And freedom, by its very nature, cuts both ways.

I wrestle with that sometimes. I try to argue with myself before I ever argue with anyone else. If a public school offers a Bible elective and then says it will also offer courses on Judaism, Buddhism, or Islam, do I have the right to be angry as a Christian? The more I think about it, the more I land on a simple conclusion: I don't think so. The same constitutional protection that guards my right to read Scripture must also guard someone else's right to read something else. If I demand liberty for myself, I must allow liberty for others. Otherwise, it isn't freedom — it's favoritism. And what humbles me most is realizing that God Himself does not coerce belief.

He commands repentance, calls for faith, and warns of judgment, yet throughout Scripture, we see choice. Joshua stood before Israel and said, "Choose this day whom you will serve."

Jesus invited, taught, loved — and even allowed people to walk away.

If God allows human volition, who am I to insist on government compulsion? The early church did not spread because Rome endorsed Christianity. It grew under pressure.

Romans 13 and First Peter were written under governments far from friendly to believers. The church's power was never political — it was truth carried by the Spirit. And history still whispers that lesson. Millions of Christians across the world have never known religious liberty. They gather quietly, sometimes at great personal risk, and yet the church often flourishes in those places. Meanwhile, in lands of full freedom, churches sometimes struggle against distraction and indifference. That alone should give us pause.

Pluralism does not automatically mean paganism. Historically, paganism referred to systems of worship detached from biblical revelation. Pluralism simply describes multiple belief systems coexisting under legal protection. It does not declare them equally true. It declares the government will not dictate belief. That distinction matters. As a simple man, I keep returning to Jesus' words: love God fully and love your neighbor as yourself. Loving my neighbor means defending his right to choose, even when I believe his choice is wrong. That doesn't require watering down the gospel. It doesn't require pretending that all roads lead to heaven. It simply means refusing to demand force where faith must be freely given.

There's a phrase I once encountered that continues to resonate with me: confident pluralism. I can live my faith boldly without trying to silence yours. I can proclaim Christ publicly while defending your right to disagree.

That isn't weakness; it's confidence in truth. Christians should cherish religious liberty, use it wisely, and live it faithfully — preaching, teaching, serving, raising families with conviction, and being salt and light.

Salt doesn't shout at the meat. Light doesn't wrestle the darkness. They simply do what they were created to do. The moment we try to force faith; we misunderstand faith itself. True worship cannot be legislated. A transformed heart cannot be manufactured by policy.

So how do we live in a pluralistic society? Perhaps more simply than we sometimes imagine. Follow Jesus wholeheartedly. Defend freedom broadly. Influence through character, service, and truth spoken with grace. Stand firm without becoming hostile. Speak clearly without becoming cruel. Because if our faith cannot thrive in freedom without coercion, then maybe we've trusted power more than the gospel.

I don't want a fragile Christianity dependent on government support. I want the kind that flourishes in truth, whether favored or opposed. Freedom for me, but also for thee — not because all beliefs are equal, but because real faith must be chosen. That's how a simple man sees it anyway. Now scoot a little closer on that porch swing… what do you think?

Jim Williams

"Let us not grow weary of doing good…"

— Galatians 6:9 (ESV)

Peace That Lasts

And let me take it one step further, because this is where the conversation gets uncomfortable. It's easy to defend freedom when it benefits me; it's far harder to defend it when it benefits someone whose beliefs I believe are wrong. That's the real test. If I only champion liberty when my side wins, then I don't truly love freedom — I love advantage. And advantage has always been a fragile thing. Power shifts. Influence shifts. History proves that over and over again. There have been seasons where Christianity held cultural power, and seasons where it didn't. There are places today where believers are the majority, and others where they are the minority. The honest question becomes: what happens when the tables turn? If we build systems that allow coercion, we must be prepared for those same systems to one day coerce us. That's not fear speaking — that's history.

Freedom is safest when it is broad, not narrow. Now, don't misunderstand me. I'm not saying truth is relative. I believe Jesus when He says, "I am the way, the truth, and the life." That claim is exclusive, clear, and unwavering. But there is a difference between holding exclusive truth and enforcing oppressive control. Jesus invited; He did not compel. He preached, healed, loved, and confronted sin, but He still allowed people to decide. Even when they decided wrongly. Even when those decisions led to His crucifixion. That kind of confidence carries remarkable weight. Jesus did not panic because Rome was in charge. He did not scramble for influence within Caesar's palace. He built a Kingdom not of this world — and that Kingdom outlasted Rome itself.

That truth steadies me deeply. Because perhaps the better question is not, "How do we make the culture behave Christian?" Rather, "How do we make the church behave Christlike?" If believers consistently lived unmistakably different lives — marked by integrity, sacrificial love, generosity, purity, humility, and courage — would we even need to argue so loudly? The early church did not change the world through legislation. They changed it through a witness. By caring for the sick during plagues. By rescuing abandoned children. By forgiving persecutors. By standing firm in truth, even when it costs them everything. That was power — not loud, but lasting.

Maybe that's where this porch conversation ultimately settles. Freedom is not the enemy of faith. Fear is. Control is. Insecurity is. If I genuinely trust that the gospel is the power of God for salvation, then I don't have to panic when other beliefs exist. I don't have to silence every opposing voice. I can stand firm, speak clearly, love boldly, and trust the Spirit to do what only He can do. Because conversion is not my assignment. Faithfulness is. And that realization humbles me, especially when I remember there was a time when I didn't fully see the truth either. Someone showed patience with me. Someone answered my questions. Someone loved me before I had everything figured out.

What if that is what I am called to be now? Not an enforcer or culture cop, but a steady witness — a neighbor who serves, a coworker who listens, a friend who speaks truth without arrogance. Freedom for me, but also for thee. Not because all roads are equal, but because love requires choice, and genuine faith cannot exist without it. So, I will keep loving Jesus, keep speaking His name, keep defending the right for others to disagree with me, and keep trusting that truth carried with grace is stronger than force.

Now that's enough heavy talk for one swing. You still sitting there? Good. Let's keep talking.

"Endurance doesn't shout— it just keeps going."

— Jim Williams

Watching the Snow Melt

Sitting on the bus this morning, riding along with nothing but time and a window to look out of, my mind wandered, as it tends to do. We're about two weeks out of that record-breaking snowfall, and at my house, it measured nearly fourteen and a half inches. Even now, after a few warmer days, there are still stubborn piles of snow holding on. They're shrinking, sure, but they haven't quite given up, especially in the shaded spots. Those lingering patches seem almost determined to stay. Watching that slow melt stirred something reflective in me. It got me thinking about the Earth itself.

There was a time, long before any of us, when this world was covered in ice. An ice age. Ice so thick and heavy it shaped the land as it slowly retreated, carving valleys, shifting rivers, leaving scars still visible if you look closely enough. And as I watched those snow piles gradually give way, it made me wonder whether we are always as quick as we should be to label what we see as unnatural. Are we witnessing something wildly out of balance, or are we sometimes watching natural processes unfolding on timescales far longer than our patience? Ice doesn't rush. It melts when conditions allow it. It yields slowly, often unevenly, lingering where the sun rarely reaches.

Now, don't misunderstand me. I believe we are called to care for what God has given us. Scripture is clear that we are stewards, caretakers rather than owners. Responsibility matters. Conservation matters. Wastefulness has never been wisdom. But I also think there is room for humility in how we interpret the world around us. Fear can be loud. Headlines can be urgent. Yet urgency does not always equal understanding.

I believe Genesis is history, not myth, not symbolic poetry detached from reality, but the foundational account of creation itself. The flood was not merely metaphorical; its echoes appear throughout the physical world. The ice age was not imaginary; its fingerprints are written across continents. God has worked through water, ice, fire, and time before. None of this surprises Him. So maybe the Earth is warming. Maybe it is still adjusting from forces set in motion long ago. Maybe human influence and natural processes are intertwined in ways we do not yet fully grasp.

I don't pretend to have definitive answers. I'm just a simple man trying to make sense of a complicated world. But as the snow continues its patient retreat — day by day, inch by inch — it reminds me that not everything requires panic. Some things call for patience. Some require humility. And some are simply worth sitting with quietly, pondering before we convince ourselves we have it all figured out.

Standing When the World Rages

I watch the world, and it's easy to feel small. Evil often seems loud, bold, and organized, while confusion and chaos feel like the background noise of everyday life. Scripture captures that picture with unsettling clarity: "The nations rage, and the peoples plot in vain." There is no denying that unity carries power. Organized unbelievers move together with purpose, while believers too often scatter, argue, or quietly hope someone else will stand. Yet God did not call His people to retreat into passivity. Babel reminds us that unity without God is dangerous, but unity under His authority is a different story altogether.

We know the ending. Revelation paints it plainly — evil will not have the last word, and Christ will ultimately triumph. But knowing the outcome does not excuse inaction. God never intended His people to fold their hands while righteousness is trampled. He calls us to stand, to speak, and to act. Jesus Himself modeled that balance. He taught patience, mercy, and love for enemies. He turned the other cheek. He prayed for those who opposed Him. But He also overturned tables, confronted deception, and responded to injustice with unmistakable authority. His life shows us that gentleness and boldness are not opposites; they are both expressions of obedience when rightly applied.

We live in a time when the unbelieving world often appears relentless and unified, pushing agendas and shaping culture with confidence. Believers, by contrast, can drift toward hesitation, fear, or silence. But we are still called to be salt and light, still called to bear witness to truth, still called to courage. Scripture reminds us there is a time for patience, a time for prayer, and a time for action.

Ecclesiastes tells us there is a season for everything under heaven, and perhaps part of spiritual wisdom is recognizing which season we are in. This is not a call to hatred or reckless anger. It is a call to righteous courage — courage rooted in love for God, anchored in truth, and guided by humility. We are called to live as peacemakers and warriors at the same time, discerning when to wait and when to stand firm. The world may be loud, unstable, and at times intimidating, but God remains sovereign. And His people are never powerless when they stand together in Him, walking faithfully, speaking truthfully, and trusting that His purposes will always prevail.

When Tolerance Ends, and Righteous Action Begins

Sometimes I sit back and watch the world and feel like I'm standing on the sidelines, trying to make sense of all the noise. The lines between right and wrong can blur so easily that it becomes dizzying, and yet Scripture continually reminds me there is a balance we are called to walk. There is a time for tolerance, for patience, for turning the other cheek as Jesus taught in Matthew 5:39. But there is also a time when righteous anger must rise, like it did when Jesus overturned the tables in the temple. The Bible is clear that the world will move through seasons of chaos and injustice. Psalm 2 tells us the nation's rage and the people's plot in vain. Revelation paints pictures of organized systems aligned against God's truth. We know the ending. We know Jesus wins. But knowing the ending does not mean we stand aside and let evil run unchecked.

God calls His people to stand, to speak, and to act where we can. When I look around, it's easy to see how organized unbelievers move with unity and precision. They gather, they plan, they push forward with shared purpose. Genesis 11 reminds us that unity itself is powerful — powerful enough that God scattered Babel when that unity moved against His will. Organized unbelief carries influence. Disorganized belief struggles to make an impact. Jesus did not hesitate to confront injustice. He overturned tables. He made noise.

He challenged deception directly. And I can't help but wonder, if Jesus walked our streets today, would He not still warn the people, expose lies, and confront systems of greed and corruption? Even knowing the outcome, He would act because truth must be declared and righteousness must be defended.

Faith was never meant to be passive. We are not called to let belief sit quietly while the world presses against God's principles. We are called to seek unity, to stay alert, and to act when righteousness is under attack. In a world that often feels upside down, God calls us to live as both peacemakers and warriors — salt that preserves, light that exposes, stewards who guard His truth.

The challenge is not choosing between gentleness and courage but knowing when each is required. May we have the wisdom to show patience when patience reflects Christ, and the courage to stand firm when courage honors Him. And through it all, may we remember our ultimate allegiance belongs to God, not man. Even though we know the ending, we are still called to stand firm, speak boldly, and act faithfully.

When We Choose Jesus Over Labels

I was sitting with a book in my lap, *God Chasers* by Tommy Tenney, when I came across the story of the Azusa Street Revival. I had heard the name before — most church folks have — but reading about it slowed me down. People from different races, different backgrounds, different languages, all gathered into a small, unimpressive building with one thing in common: they were hungry for God. Not for a brand. Not for a platform. Not for a denominational badge. Hungry.

What happened there wasn't polished or predictable. By most accounts, it was messy. Yet it was undeniably powerful. It reminded me of Acts 2, where Scripture says they devoted themselves to teaching, fellowship, prayer, and awe came upon every soul. Awe. That word lingered with me because awe is something you cannot manufacture, schedule, or market.

So, I did what a curious, simple man tends to do — I started digging. Azusa wasn't alone. There was the Welsh Revival. There was the Toronto Blessing. Even today, revival gatherings and healing movements surface across the world. And one word kept surfacing around many of those movements: Pentecostal. And there is again — a label. Pentecostal. Baptist. Methodist. Charismatic. Each one carries history, convictions, traditions, and sometimes walls. That realization made me pause and ask some uncomfortable questions. Can we chase the Holy Spirit so intensely that we risk missing Jesus?

Can we become so fascinated with gifts — tongues, prophecies, healing — that we forget the Giver? Paul warned about imbalance when he wrote that speaking in tongues without love becomes noise. Power without love becomes hollow. Experience without grounding becomes instability.

I don't wrestle with those questions as a critic, but as a hungry man. I've tasted moments of God's presence in my own life that I can't explain away — moments where Scripture burned brighter and prayer felt thick with His nearness. And I want more of that. But I also want the truth. I was raised Baptist in northeastern North Carolina. We believed in the Trinity. We believed in the Holy Spirit. But if I'm honest, He didn't seem to get much room. We spoke often of the Father. We preached boldly about the Son. The Spirit sometimes felt like the quiet relative we acknowledged but didn't fully lean into. Yet Jesus Himself said we would receive power when the Holy Spirit came upon us — not conference power or once-a-year revival power, but power for everyday living.

Reading about Azusa, Wales, and Toronto, I see people who made room — room for repentance, room for prayer, room for God to move outside the tidy outline. And here's what I'm slowly realizing: the issue isn't Pentecostal versus Baptist. The issue isn't expressive versus reserved. The issue is what happens when we choose labels over Jesus. Jesus didn't hand out denominational stickers. He simply said, "Follow Me." That's it. Follow. I can honor my Baptist roots, love sound doctrine, cling tightly to Scripture, and still welcome the Holy Spirit into the daily corners of my life. Those things are not enemies. They belong together.

Revival doesn't start with a stage; it starts with surrender. It doesn't begin with lights and music; it begins with repentance. It isn't built on emotional hype; it's built on hunger.

Hunger isn't inherited from denomination or borrowed from a movement. It's deeply personal. And maybe revival isn't something we visit every few decades. Maybe it's something we live in daily — when we choose Jesus over labels, pursue truth while welcoming the Spirit, hold conviction without building walls, and remember the goal was never to defend a tribe but to follow a Savior. A simple man doesn't need to pick a camp. He just needs to stay close to Christ. And maybe, just maybe, if we chose Jesus over labels more often, we'd see less division, more awe, and a Church that looks a little more like Acts 2 and a little less like competing teams. That's what's been sitting with me on the porch. What about you?

"He restores my soul."

— Psalm 23:3 (ESV)

When God's Justice Feels Bigger Than Mine

Some thoughts don't knock politely; they simply sit down heavily on your chest. This was one of those days. I kept circling back to a verse I've heard my whole life: "Vengeance is Mine," says the Lord. I'll be honest — those words land differently when you've tasted injustice, when you've been lied about, overlooked, wronged, or misunderstood. There is something deeply human in us that long for balance to be restored. We want the scales tipped back. We want consequences delivered. We want to see wrong made right, preferably on our timeline. That pull toward fairness feels natural, but so do pride, anger, and the quiet desire for revenge. Somewhere between justice and vengeance, a simple man must pause and ask: what belongs to me, and what belongs to God?

"Vengeance is Mine" does not mean God ignores evil or shrugs at wrongdoing. It means justice is above my pay grade. God is perfectly just, yet He also sees what I cannot see. He sees motives I cannot read, wounds I did not witness, and brokenness that hides behind behavior. That is where things become uncomfortable, because if I'm honest, there are moments when I don't want redemption for the person who hurt me — I want consequences, immediate ones. There is a man I know, someone I struggle to like, and every time his name comes up, something tightens in me. My flesh would feel strangely satisfied watching him face the music. But that is not my role. That is where the verse echoes again, steady and unyielding: "Vengeance is Mine."

Maybe God's justice is larger than punishment alone. Sometimes it may seem like exposure, sometimes discipline, and sometimes redemption. What if God's way of conquering evil is not only crushing it but transforming it? What if His vengeance includes reclaiming lost souls? That thought humbles me quickly, because if I'm honest, I am one of those souls He reclaimed. There were seasons in my own life when I was the offender — blind, stubborn, and wrong. If someone had demanded justice on my timeline, I would not have liked the outcome. But God showed mercy. Justice and mercy met at the cross. God did not ignore wrong; He absorbed it. He did not excuse sin; He paid for it.

So, when my heart burns for fairness, I find myself stepping back and whispering, Lord, I trust Your scales more than mine. You see the whole story. You know what discipline looks like. You know what restoration looks like. Letting go of vengeance does not mean pretending nothing happened; it means handing it to the only Judge who can hold justice and mercy without dropping either.

That is hard. It can feel weak at first. But perhaps it is a strength. Perhaps trusting God with justice is one of the most mature steps a believer can take. Because when I insist on personal vengeance, I shrink God down to my emotional size, and He is far bigger than that. His justice is wiser than my anger, His mercy deeper than my frustration, and His plan may include saving the very person I struggle to forgive. Isn't that our walk, after all — learning again and again that God's ways are higher than ours, and sometimes the most faithful thing a simple man can do is step back, release the scorecard, and trust that God's justice is not only real, but far greater than mine.

When Tradition Speaks Louder Than Scripture

The longer I walk with Jesus, the more I realize something that makes me both smile and squirm a little: a whole lot of what we "know" in church culture isn't actually written in Scripture — it's tradition. Now, before anyone tightens up, hear me clearly. Tradition isn't the enemy. But tradition can get loud, and if we're not careful, it can start speaking louder than the Word itself. Take Christmas, for example.

We celebrate Jesus' birth on December 25th, and I genuinely love Christmas — the lights, the hymns, the gathering of family, the intentional focus on Christ. But if you read carefully, Scripture never gives us a date. Shepherds watching their flocks by night usually point to warmer months, not the dead of winter. Is celebrating December 25th wrong? Of course not. But the date is tradition, not revelation.

Then there's the nativity scene — beautiful, peaceful, and deeply familiar. Yet Matthew tells us the Magi didn't show up the night Jesus was born. They first went to Jerusalem asking about the King, and by the time they found Him, Jesus was in a house, not a stable. Herod's decree involving boys two years and under suggests Jesus may have been a toddler. Still, we line them up beside the manger every year. Is that sinful? No. But it isn't Scripture either. And once you start noticing the difference between tradition and text, the list grows quickly.

Mary riding a donkey to Bethlehem? The Bible never says she did. An innkeeper turning them away? Scripture never mentions one. Eve eating an apple? It simply says fruit.

The Magi being kings? They're called wise men, not royalty. Hell as Satan's throne room? The Bible describes it as a place of punishment, not his kingdom.

Angels as soft, winged figurines with halos? Most angels appear as ordinary men, and the winged beings described in Scripture are awe-inspiring, even unsettling. Satan as a red cartoon villain with horns and a pitchfork? That image comes from art, not the biblical text. Even phrases like "God helps those who help themselves" carry the weight of familiarity without ever appearing in Scripture.

None of these traditions are necessarily harmful. They can make holidays joyful, help children visualize stories, and bring rhythm and beauty to church life. But they do remind me of something important: it is incredibly easy to inherit beliefs that never actually came from God, only from repetition. And repetition is powerful. If you hear something long enough, it begins to feel sacred, even if it never came from Scripture. Maybe part of spiritual maturity is learning to separate what God actually said from what we've simply always heard — not to tear down tradition or mock it, but to make sure tradition never replaces truth.

Jesus Himself had strong words for religious leaders who elevated tradition above God's Word, and that warning still echoes. Because when tradition speaks louder than Scripture, drift is almost inevitable. Not intentional drift. Not rebellious drift. Just gradual, quiet movement away from the anchor. And as a simple man in a complicated world, I don't want to drift. I don't want my convictions shaped by paintings, pageants, or cultural memory alone. I want them shaped by the text. Returning to the Word doesn't make us cold; it makes us anchored.

It doesn't strip away joy; it deepens it, because our joy becomes rooted in what is true. At the end of the day, I'm simply trying to make sure the voice shaping my faith is His Word — not just someone else's story repeated often enough to feel holy.

"Sometimes healing is slow—

but it's still happening."

— Jim Williams

Just Reach for the Kanaph

It's one thing to talk about faith. It's another thing to actually live it. If I'm being honest—and if you're honest with yourself—you've struggled with that too. There have been moments in my life where reaching out in faith felt uncomfortable, where it meant standing out, where it meant not blending in with the crowd. And if you've ever been there, you know exactly what I'm talking about. Because sometimes it's not just the world that makes you feel that way. Sometimes… It's the church.

I remember in my early walk with Christ, I spent a lot of time watching other believers—listening, learning, trying to figure out what this life was supposed to look like. And if I'm being real, I found myself imitating what I thought Christianity was supposed to be. But somewhere along the way, I got caught up in things that didn't sit right in my spirit—legalism, rituals, traditions that felt more like performance than relationship. I remember thinking, "If all these Christians are doing this, it can't be wrong… can it?" But deep down, something in my soul kept whispering, "This isn't it."

It took me a while to understand something simple but powerful: just because something is common doesn't mean it's Christ. Just because something is practiced doesn't mean it's alive.

And just like I wrote earlier about that tree on the mountain, I realized I was different—not just different from the world, but different in the church too. And for a while, that made me feel out of place.

But now I see it differently. God had given me eyes to see, ears to hear, and the Holy Spirit to guide me—not to follow the crowd, but to follow Him. Now hear me—this isn't me saying traditions are wrong. There's beauty in them when they point to Christ. But when they replace Him, when they become the focus instead of the relationship, we miss the whole point. Because following Jesus was never meant to feel like a performance. It was meant to be a pursuit.

We also must be careful here, because the truth is, many people in the church genuinely believe they are doing what's right. They're not trying to lead people astray. They're trying to be faithful. They're trying to honor God the best way they know how. And if we're honest, they'll fight for it, stand on it, even die on that hill if it comes to it. But history has already shown us something we can't ignore. The Pharisees—the religious leaders, the very people who studied the Scriptures, taught in the synagogues, and lived as close to the law as anyone possibly could—they missed Him. They knew the words. They knew the traditions. They knew the law. But when the Messiah stood right in front of them, they didn't recognize Him.

Now hear me clearly—this isn't about bashing the church. I love the church. This is about something deeper than that. This is about making sure we don't make the same mistake twice. Because it's possible to be around the things of God and still miss the heart of God.

It's possible to follow the structure and miss the Savior. It's possible to know all the right practices and still not reach for Him.

And then one day, I saw something in Scripture that stopped me in my tracks. In the very last book of the Old Testament, Malachi 4:2 says, "The Sun of righteousness shall rise with healing in His wings." That word "wings" in Hebrew is *kanaph*. And *kanaph* doesn't just mean wings like a bird—it also means edge, corner, the fringe of a garment, the place where the tassels hang. So, Malachi wasn't just speaking poetically. He was pointing to something very real. Healing wouldn't just come from Him—it would be found in the very edges of His covering, in His *kanaph*.

Now fast forward hundreds of years to Mark chapter 5. A woman who had been bleeding for twelve years—tired, broken, outcast. According to the law, she shouldn't even be in the crowd, but she presses through anyway. And she says something that changes everything: "If I can just touch His garment…" Not His hand. Not His voice. Not even His face. Just the edge. Just the fringe. Just the *kanaph*. And the moment she touches it, she's healed.

Now here's the question that stops me: did she know? Did she know what Malachi had written? Did she understand that healing was spoken to be in His *kanaph*? Did she recognize that this was the Messiah? Scripture doesn't tell us. But it tells us something even more important—she had faith. Jesus didn't say, "My garment healed you." He said, "Daughter, your faith has made you well."

And that's where this gets real for me. Because I know what it feels like to stand in a crowd, even a church crowd—and feel like I don't quite belong.

To see everyone moving one way, and something in me saying, "Just reach for Jesus." Not the system. Not the routine. Not what everyone else is doing. Just Him.

That woman didn't wait to have a perfect understanding. She didn't try to blend in. She didn't stand back and analyze. She just reached. And whether she fully understood the prophecy or not, she reached in the exact place God had spoken about centuries before.

Maybe that's the lesson for us. We don't have to have it all figured out. We don't have to look like everyone else. We don't have to follow the crowd just because it's the crowd. Maybe we just need to have enough faith to reach. Because healing isn't found in fitting in, it's found in Him. And sometimes all it takes is reaching for the very place He promised healing would be… the *kanaph*.

Still a Simple Man

After walking through politics, nations, labels, peace, and discernment, I always seem to circle back to something simple. I am not called to fix the world. I am called to follow Jesus inside it. That realization has taken some pressure off my shoulders. The weight of trying to solve everything, arguing everything, correcting everything—it's heavy. And it's not mine to carry.

Micah 6:8 keeps coming back to me: act justly, love mercy, walk humbly. Three short phrases, but they hold a lifetime of direction. Justice without mercy becomes harsh and cold. Mercy without truth becomes hollow and weak. Humility is what keeps both steady. Humility reminds me that I don't see the full picture, that I'm capable of being wrong, that grace was extended to me long before I learned how to extend it to others.

This world is complicated. Every issue seems layered. Every headline pulls at emotion. Every conversation can feel like a battlefield if we let it. But Christ is not complicated. He is steady. His character doesn't shift with the news cycle. His truth doesn't wobble with public opinion. His grace doesn't dry up when culture changes.

If I anchor myself to Him, I don't have to be tossed around by every cultural wave. I can stand firm without becoming rigid. I can speak clearly without becoming cruel. I can care deeply without becoming consumed. That balance doesn't come from personality or intelligence—it comes from staying close to Him.

I am still just a simple man. The world hasn't gotten less complicated. If anything, it feels more tangled than ever. But grace is still sufficient. The cross still stands. The Spirit still guides. And when I remember that my calling is not to control the world but to walk faithfully in it, direction changes everything.

Reading Between the Lines

Pull up a chair for a minute. Let's talk about this Book.

For a long time, I was familiar with the Bible the way you're familiar with a back road. I knew it was there. I'd driven it a few times. I could probably point out a landmark or two. But I didn't really study it. I didn't slow down long enough to notice what was sitting between the lines. It was present in my life, but it wasn't shaping my life.

Now? It's different.

The older I get, and the more complicated this world feels, the more I find myself leaning into it. Not out of habit. Not because that's what I was raised to do. Not out of tradition. But out of hunger. There's something about watching the world spin faster and louder that makes you crave something steady.

Some folks see the Bible as just another old book. Ink on paper. Stories passed down. Maybe even outdated. And I get that. If you approach it like a history textbook, that's probably all you'll see. Facts. Names. Places. Events. You read it, close it, and move on.

But sit with it long enough… and something shifts.

It's not just stories. It's a tapestry. Sixty-six books written over centuries by different authors from different cultures—shepherds, kings, fishermen, doctors. And somehow, through all of that, it tells one unfolding story. One thread runs from beginning to end. That alone ought to make you pause.

My pastor says something that's stuck with me for years. He calls it "understanding the white space."

The white space. Not just the words printed in black, but the space between them. The pauses. The cultural details. The towns you can barely pronounce. The festivals you usually skim past. The silence between verses was where life was still happening.

That's where it gets rich.

That's where Abraham's walk feels longer. That's where David's failures feel heavier. That's where Jesus' pauses feel intentional. When you start digging into the white space, the Bible stops being flat. It starts breathing.

I think one reason people struggle with it is that we don't always help them see the context. We hand them verses without background. Commands without culture. Stories without setting. No wonder it feels distant. But when you realize these towns were real places, these were real families with real dysfunction, these festivals had meaning, and these conflicts had historical connections. It feels less like a myth and more like a mirror.

And the more I study, the more convinced I become: this Book isn't surviving by accident. Generation after generation has tried to dismiss it, rewrite it, silence it, discredit it. And yet here it stands. Still read. Still debated. Still changing lives.

Now, let me say something gently. A lot of people who don't believe approach the Bible already determined to prove it wrong. And if you come to it like a prosecutor, you'll probably find something to accuse. But I've found that if you come to it with an open heart instead of a clenched fist, it reads differently. It doesn't just sit there waiting to be examined. It reads you back.

And while we're here, don't judge the Bible by God's people. We're flawed. We mess up. We misrepresent Him sometimes. We say things we shouldn't. We act in ways that don't line up. But God's Word? That's steady.

There's a difference between Logos—the written Word—and Rhema—when that written Word becomes alive in you. When a verse you've read ten times suddenly reads you. When it moves from ink on a page to conviction in your chest.

That's when it changes you.

And here's the simple part of all this. Jesus boiled the whole thing down to two commands: love the Lord your God with all your heart, soul, and mind, and love your neighbor as yourself. You live that out—really live it—and you won't go too far wrong.

Can you imagine what this world would look like if we actually did that? Not posted about it. Not argued about it. Not debated denominations, preferences, and styles. Just loved God fully and loved people well.

That's not complicated theology. That's porch theology.

And I'm just a simple man, still learning, still digging in the white space, still letting this Book shape me instead of the world around me. If you haven't opened it in a while, maybe dust it off. Not to win an argument. Not to prove a point. Just to sit with it.

You might find it's been waiting for you.

Jim Williams

"If we confess our sins…"

— 1 John 1:9 (ESV)

The Complicated Blessing

As a simple man in a complicated world, I've read the story of Jacob and Esau more than once and found myself shaking my head. Two brothers, one blessing, and a father were caught in the middle. If you've ever spent time in Genesis 27, you know it isn't a neat, polished story. It's messy in the most human way — deception, favoritism, manipulation. Jacob tricks his father, Isaac. Rebekah schemes behind the scenes. Esau burns with anger. And a family fracture over something that was meant to be sacred. It's the kind of story that makes you uncomfortable because it doesn't feel ancient — it feels familiar.

And every time I read it, I find myself thanking God. Not because of the deceit, and certainly not because of the brokenness, but because my story with my brothers didn't unfold that way. I didn't grow up in the same house as them. They were building memories with our dad while I was on the outside looking in. They shared traditions I wasn't part of, stories I wasn't present for, and experiences I can never fully step into. In some ways, it would have been easy for that to harden into bitterness. It is easy for distance to turn into competition. Easy for absence to become resentment.

But it didn't, especially with Sammy. We didn't grow up side by side, yet we didn't grow up fighting either. There was no war over attention, no silent rivalry over blessings or position. What we had once considered extraordinary became normal for us. We accepted the shape of our story without turning it into a battlefield. Looking back now, I see that for what it truly was — a blessing of a different kind.

Genesis 27 shows me what can happen when brothers compete instead of accepting, when favoritism replaces fairness, and when deception erodes trust. Yes, Jacob received the blessing, but it came at a cost. Esau's heartbreak was real. The division was real. The consequences were real. Yet even inside that dysfunction, God's plan continued to move forward. That's the part that steadies me. God's sovereignty does not depend on human perfection. His purposes are not fragile. Even through broken families, flawed decisions, and painful consequences, His will stands.

Isaac's blessing over Jacob still unfolded, not because every action in that story was honorable, but because God's design was already in motion. That humbles me. It reminds me of Isaiah's words: "For as the heavens are higher than the earth, so are My ways higher than your ways and My thoughts than your thoughts." There are dynamics within families we do not fully understand, seasons that feel uneven, and roles we never asked to play. Some are favored. Some feel forgotten. Some are inside the house. Some grow up outside of it.

But God sees the whole picture.

And here's what I've learned as a simple man: you don't have to fight your brother to receive what God has for you. If it is truly yours, God will bring it in His time and His way. If it is not, no amount of scheming will ever make it peaceful. I'm grateful my story with my brothers didn't mirror Jacob and Esau's. It wasn't perfect, and it certainly wasn't storybook, but it wasn't war.

Sometimes the greatest blessing isn't in gaining what someone else holds.

Sometimes the blessing is simply peace; peace between brothers is no small gift.

When Conviction Falls Asleep

There's an old saying that's stuck with me for years: you put a frog in a pan of cold water, set it on the stove, and slowly turn up the heat. The frog doesn't panic, doesn't leap — he adapts. The water warms so gradually that he convinces himself everything is fine. He adjusts. He tolerates. He settles. Until it's too late. Now, whether that's good science or not isn't really the point. The picture is what stays with me. Because when I look at Christianity today, I can't help but wonder if we've been sitting in warm water longer than we realize.

Most believers didn't wake up one morning and decide to throw out Scripture. It didn't happen like that. The heat came up slowly. A verse softened here. A hard truth was avoided there. "Don't judge" became louder than "repent." We were told — rightly — that God loves everyone, but then that truth was stretched so thin it began erasing holiness, obedience, and the call to be set apart. Jesus absolutely loves everyone. That's the heartbeat of the gospel. But loving everyone is not the same as approving everything. Jesus forgave sinners, yet He also said, "Go and sin no more." He ate with tax collectors, yet He made it clear He came to call sinners to repentance. He showed mercy without lowering the standard.

Somewhere along the way, tolerance began replacing transformation. We've been told Jesus saves everyone, but Scripture speaks of salvation through belief, repentance, and following Him. We've been told not to judge, yet Jesus called us to judge rightly, not abandon discernment altogether.

We've been told love means affirmation, yet Jesus said those He loves, He corrects. That's not harsh — that's holy. I think the real danger isn't loud rebellion; it's quiet adaptation. It's not someone openly shaking their fist at God. It's someone slowly redefining obedience until it barely resembles what Scripture says.

The frog doesn't perish because the water suddenly boils. He perishes because he never recognizes when it's time to jump. As a simple man trying to follow Christ in a complicated world, I keep returning to Jesus' words: "You are the salt of the earth" and "You are the light of the world." Salt doesn't adapt to the meat — it preserves it. Light doesn't blend into darkness — it exposes it. If salt loses its saltiness, it becomes useless. If light hides, the room stays dark. God's love is steady. His grace is deep. But His truth does not shift with cultural temperature. Holiness does not become outdated. Repentance does not become optional. Obedience does not become extreme.

Maybe the most honest and necessary question we can ask ourselves is this: Have I adapted where I should have stood? Have I softened where I should have surrendered? Have I confused compassion with compromise? There is nothing wrong with loving people. There is nothing wrong with kindness. But if the cost of peace is truth, the water may be getting hotter than we realize.

Sometimes faithfulness looks like standing still while culture moves, and sometimes it looks like having the courage to step away from comfort before comfort becomes compromised. A simple man doesn't need to shout. He just needs to stay awake. Because the heat rarely rises all at once, and truth does not change simply because the room grows warmer.

Stepping Out When the Path Is Unknown

Hmmm… Abraham. When we say his name, we say it with weight — father of faith, patriarch, promise-bearer. But before he was any of that, he was simply a man. A man with a home, a routine, familiar roads beneath his feet, family close by, land he understood. And then God spoke. "Leave your country, your people, your father's household — and go to the land I will show you." Not the land I have shown you. The land I will show you.

That difference matters. Genesis 12 reads calmly on the page, but if you slow it down, it's staggering. Leave everything you know for a promise you cannot yet see. No map. No timeline. No guarantee of comfort. Just a voice and a promise: "I will make you into a great nation… I will bless you… and all peoples on earth will be blessed through you." What a promise. What a responsibility. And Abraham went.

Let's not romanticize it too much, though. Abraham wasn't flawless. He stumbled, doubted, and at times tried to help God fulfill the promise in his own way. But when the call came, he stepped. That's faith. Not perfection, but movement. We live in a complicated world, too. We may not be asked to pack up tents and cross deserts, but we are asked to leave comfort zones — to forgive when resentment feels easier, to give when hoarding feels safer, to speak truth when silence seems less costly, to obey before outcomes are visible. And often, God still speaks in much the same way: "Go to the land I will show you." Meaning we don't see it all at once. Step first. See you later. That's the part that stretches a simple man like me.

We like clarity. We like plans. We like knowing how things turn out. But faith has never been built on full disclosure. It's built on trust in the One who calls. Jesus Himself spoke of Abraham, saying, "Your father Abraham rejoiced that he would see My day; he saw it and was glad." Somehow, through promise and prophecy, Abraham glimpsed something far greater than land or descendants. He saw redemption coming. He didn't see the cross clearly. He didn't know the name of Jesus. But he trusted God's promise enough to rejoice in what he couldn't fully understand. That challenges me deeply, because there are days when I struggle to trust even what I can see. Abraham trusted what he couldn't.

What if we lived like that? Not waiting for perfect clarity, not demanding every detail, but taking the next faithful step. Maybe the path doesn't unfold all at once. Maybe it reveals itself one act of obedience at a time. The world around us is complicated. Decisions feel heavy. Brokenness swirls like a dust storm. But God's call remains remarkably simple: trust Me, follow Me, step. He is faithful. He was faithful to Abraham, faithful through generations, faithful enough to send the blessing promised long ago — Jesus Himself. And if He kept that promise across centuries, He can surely keep the promises He's made to you and me. Maybe faith isn't about knowing the whole road. Maybe it's about trusting the One who does. A simple man doesn't need the full map — just enough courage to take the next step.

If God Has You Waiting… Be a Waiter and Serve

For most of my life, it has felt like a waiting game. Not the quiet, peaceful kind of waiting, but the kind where you think, *this is it… this is where I'm supposed to be*, only to have the door close just as quickly as it opened. I've stepped into moments that felt right, only to watch them slip away. And if I'm being honest, after enough of those seasons, something starts to settle in your spirit that doesn't belong there. A quiet thought begins to whisper, *maybe you're just not good enough*. It doesn't shout. It doesn't make a scene. It just lingers.

There has always been something in me that wanted to serve. Not for recognition, not for position, but simply to be used. Isaiah 6:8 has stayed close to my heart: "Whom shall I send, and who will go for us?" And my answer has always been the same—*Here I am. Send me.* I didn't care where. I didn't care what it looked like. I just wanted to be part of what God was doing. But the tension came when those opportunities didn't last. Doors would open and close. Jobs would come and go. Opportunities I felt ready for never even gave me a chance. And I didn't understand it.

There came a moment not long ago when I found myself asking God again, *What are you doing? Where is this going?* And in that quiet place, something settled into my spirit as clearly as anything I've ever known *I will put you in a place that man would not put you, and man will not take it away.* At the time, I didn't fully understand it. I didn't know what that place would look like or how I would ever get there.

But looking back now, I can see that it didn't come the way I expected. It didn't come through a title or a position. It came through obedience in small places.

It showed up in a classroom at fifty-four years old, learning how to write. It showed up teaching kids at church, trying to explain God's truth in a way a child could understand. It showed up riding a bus with exceptional and behavioral children, serving in a role most people would overlook. Nothing big. Nothing flashy. Just showing up and serving where God had already placed me. And somewhere in the middle of that, my understanding of waiting began to change.

Isaiah 40:31 says, "But they who wait for the Lord shall renew their strength…" Waiting isn't wasted. It is where God strengthens you. It is where He shapes you. It is where He prepares you for what you cannot yet see. And sometimes the reason the waiting feels so long is that the work He is doing runs deeper than we realize. I began to understand that the real question isn't just *why am I waiting?* The better question is, *what am I doing while I wait?*

Jesus said in Mark 10:45, "For even the Son of Man came not to be served but to serve…" If that was His posture, then what should ours be? Waiting was never meant to be passive. It was never meant to be sitting still, hoping something changes. It was meant to be active. Faithful. Intentional. Serving where you are. Serving those who are in front of you. Showing up even when it feels like nothing is changing. Galatians 6:9 reminds us, "Let us not grow weary of doing good, for in due season we will reap, if we do not give up." That's the part that stretches you, because the waiting can wear you down. The silence can make you question everything. But God is not absent in the waiting. He is working in it.

I don't have all the answers, but I know this—God knows how to place you exactly where you need to be, in a place no man could give you and no man can take away. And when that moment comes, you begin to see clearly that the waiting was never punishment. It was preparation. It was God doing something in you that could not be done any other way.

From the Porch, if God has you waiting right now, don't sit still. Pick up a towel. Find someone to serve. Stay faithful in what is right in front of you. Because God may be doing His deepest work in your life in the very season you almost walked away from.

"Honesty with God is where change begins."

— Jim Williams

Preparing the Way, Being John the Baptist Today

I've been sitting under our pastor's teaching through the book of Matthew, and something he said this week stopped me in my tracks. Not because it was complicated, but because it was simple — and sometimes the simplest truths are the ones we overlook the longest. He said, "As followers of Christ today… we are John the Baptist." Now I've read about John my whole life. The wild man in the wilderness, clothed in camel's hair, living on locusts and wild honey, the voice crying out in the desert calling people to repent. In my mind, he was always a historical figure — important, yes — but finished, his role complete once Jesus stepped onto the public stage. But I'd never really looked at him this way before.

John's entire life was preparation. He didn't point people to himself, didn't build a personal brand, and didn't polish an image. He cleared the road. "Repent, for the kingdom of heaven is at hand." He was a voice, not the Word, a signpost, not the destination. And when Jesus arrived, John spoke some of the most freeing words a servant can say: "He must increase, but I must decrease." That's clarity. Then Jesus lived, died, rose again, and before He ascended, He gave what we call the Great Commission — go, make disciples, baptize, teach. Not to replace Him. Not to become Him. But to point to Him. That's when something clicked for me in a way it never had before.

John prepared people for Jesus' first coming. We prepare people for His second. Different moments in history, same mission.

John called people to repentance, and so do we — not the loud, condemning version that pushes people away, but the honest kind that reminds us the world isn't our savior, comfort isn't our god, and we are not nearly as self-sufficient as we like to believe. He baptized. We baptize. He pointed to the Lamb of God. We still do. He was a voice crying out in the wilderness. We are voices crying out in a loud, distracted, complicated world. The Great Commission isn't just a church task list; it's the continuation of that same mission: prepare the way, make straight the paths, help people recognize Jesus before He appears again.

That realization carries weight, but it also brings clarity. This faith isn't about building platforms, looking polished, or growing influence for ourselves. It's about faithfulness — about pointing, preparing, and living in such a way that our lives whisper, and sometimes boldly declare, "He is coming. Are you ready?" I'm just a simple man in a complicated world, but that truth makes the call of Jesus feel both heavier and clearer. We aren't merely waiting around for heaven; we are participating in God's unfolding plan right now, preparing the way for a King who is returning. And like John, may we be willing to decrease, willing to look a little strange in the world's eyes, willing to be voices rather than the headline. Because the goal was never for people to notice us. The goal was always to make sure they see Him.

When God's House Becomes Our Distraction

There are days when the noise feels louder than my faith. Bills, deadlines, headlines, opinions, endless scrolling, all pile up. As a simple man in a complicated world, I sometimes feel that weight pressing in, and if I'm not careful, the noise starts blurring what actually matters. That's why Mark 11 stopped me. Jesus walks into the temple, the very place meant to represent God's dwelling among His people, and what does He find? Tables, coins, merchants, business, profit — activity everywhere, but not the kind that belonged there. Scripture says He overturned the tables of the money changers and drove out those buying and selling, declaring, "My house will be called a house of prayer for all nations, but you have made it a den of robbers." That's strong language, and it wasn't a loss of control. It was a controlled authority. Not temper, but holiness.

As I read that scene, I couldn't help but turn the spotlight inward, because the New Testament tells us something deeply sobering, we are the temple now. God's Spirit dwells within us. And suddenly the question becomes uncomfortable — what have I allowed to set up shop in the place meant for prayer? Success can set up a table. Comfort can set up a table. Pride can set up a table. Even good things — ministry, busyness, responsibility — can crowd out quiet communion with God. It's entirely possible to be active in church and still neglect the presence of God. The temple in Jerusalem didn't become a marketplace overnight. It drifted. Gradually. And drift is rarely loud; it's subtle. A little less prayer.

It was a little more distracting. A little less time in the Word. A little more chasing what feels urgent. Until one day, the space meant for communion feels crowded.

But here's what steadies me. Jesus didn't walk into the temple and abandon it. He cleansed it. His overturning of tables wasn't destruction for its own sake — it was restoration. He was reclaiming the purpose of that sacred space. "My house will be called a house of prayer." Not profit. Not performance. Prayer. And maybe that's the invitation for us. Not condemnation — invitation. Are there tables in my heart that need flipping? Are there habits quietly stealing time meant for God? Are there attitudes — resentment, envy, pride — that have taken up residence? Jesus doesn't merely expose the clutter; He offers grace to cleanse it. He doesn't point out the distraction and walks away. He calls us back to purpose.

In a world full of chaos, perhaps the most radical thing we can do is protect sacred space. Turn off the noise. Open the Word. Pray without multitasking. Pause long enough to let God search the heart. A temple doesn't stay holy by accident. It's kept that way through attention, surrender, and regular clearing. As a simple man, I don't need dramatic spiritual experiences every day, but I do need a clean heart — a place where prayer still has priority, where God's presence isn't competing with my distractions. Because when Jesus cleanses the temple, it isn't to shame us. It's to restore what it was always meant to be — a dwelling place for Him. And in a complicated world, that kind of inner stillness may be the most powerful witness we have.

When God's Plan Outlasts Our Confusion

Some days the world feels like one big unsolved riddle. Leaders argue nations shift, economies shake, and people carry a quiet anxiety they can't quite name. If I'm honest, there are moments when I feel a little like Nebuchadnezzar — troubled by something I can sense but can't fully explain. Daniel 2 came back to me today. A pagan king has a dream that unsettles him to the core. He knows it matters, knows it carries weight, but he can't interpret it.

So, he calls in the smartest minds in the kingdom — magicians, enchanters, astrologers — and they're stuck. They can't tell him the dream, much less its meaning. That feels strangely familiar. We live in an age flooded with information, experts on every channel, opinions filling every screen, yet confusion still seems to reign. We try to interpret life through our own wisdom, our own systems, our own reasoning, and sometimes it feels like we're just spinning our wheels.

Then Daniel steps forward, not with arrogance or self-promotion, but with something far simpler. He prays. He gathers his friends, asks for mercy from the God of heaven, and waits. And God reveals the mystery. The dream is of a great statue — head of gold, chest of silver, belly of bronze, legs of iron, feet mixed with clay — powerful kingdoms, impressive and towering.

But then comes the unexpected turn: a stone, cut out without human hands, strikes the statue, and the entire structure crumbles. Gold, silver, bronze, iron — gone like chaff in the wind. That stone, however, grows. It becomes a mountain that fills the whole earth.

Daniel explains it plainly: the statue represents earthly kingdoms — powerful, yes, but temporary. The stone represents God's kingdom — eternal, unstoppable, not built by human strength or vulnerable to collapse.

That truth settles something in me. The world often feels like that statue — massive systems, global powers, cultural movements that look unshakable. And as a simple man, it's easy to feel small standing in front of all that. But Daniel 2 whispers something steady: it doesn't matter how tall the statue looks. God's plan outlasts it. Every empire has an expiration date. Every system built on human pride eventually cracks. But the kingdom of God grows — sometimes quietly, but relentlessly. And perhaps the most comforting part of the story is this: Daniel didn't panic; he prayed. He didn't lean solely on his own understanding; he sought God. The same God who revealed mysteries then is still sovereign now. He still sees the end from the beginning. He still knows how every statue falls. He is still building His kingdom stone by stone.

So, what do we do when confusion swirls, and the world feels unstable? Maybe it's simpler than we make it. Pray. Seek Him. Ask for wisdom. Take the next faithful step. Daniel didn't know the entire future when he first bowed his head; he simply trusted the One who did. And here is the steady hope that anchors a restless heart: the stone becomes a mountain. Jesus wins — not sometimes, not barely, but always.

Even when life feels messy, when injustice seems loud, when the statue looks bigger than our courage, God's plan outlasts our confusion. His kingdom is not fragile.

It is growing. And when the dust settles, and the statues fall, the mountain remains.

Jim Williams

"There is therefore now no condemnation…"

— Romans 8:1 (ESV)

\

Finding Redemption

Before we chase stars and before we wrestle with eternity, there's something else we must admit: life is complicated. Some days it feels like the world is spinning faster than I can keep up. Headlines shout, opinions collide, and sin doesn't even try to hide anymore. If I stare at it too long, I start to feel small — small, outnumbered, unsure. That's usually when I find myself opening my Bible. Not because it suddenly makes everything simple, but because it makes everything steady.

I was reading Genesis 6 the other day, the part just before the flood, and one verse stopped me cold: "The Lord saw how great the wickedness of the human race had become on the earth, and that every inclination of the thoughts of the human heart was only evil all the time." Only evil. All the time. Sit with that for a moment. We often think our generation has cornered the market on darkness, that culture has never been more unstable or morally confused. But Genesis paints a picture so bleak it almost feels suffocating. And yet, right there in the middle of that darkness sits one quiet, hope-filled sentence: "But Noah found favor in the eyes of the Lord."

That little phrase carries more reassurance than a thousand headlines. Noah wasn't flawless, superhuman, or sinless. He was a man who trusted God in a crooked generation. And God made a way — an ark in the middle of chaos, salvation in the middle of judgment, a door of grace before the rain ever began to fall.

That pattern should sound familiar, because it echoes across Scripture. The world feels overwhelming sometimes. Sin feels loud. Corruption feels normal.

And despite all our efforts, we can't ultimately fix it with politics, arguments, or better systems. But God makes a way.

John 3:16 says it plainly: "For God so loved the world that He gave His one and only Son." Loved the world — not the cleaned-up version, not the improved version, but the broken one. Just like in Noah's day, redemption didn't rise from humanity upward; it came from God downward. The ark was God's idea. The cross was God's idea. Grace always is. And here's what I'm learning, slowly and sometimes stubbornly: darkness doesn't cancel grace. It sets the stage for it.

When everything around you feels unstable, it doesn't mean God has stepped away. It may simply mean He is doing something only He can do. Noah didn't stop the flood. He trusted the instructions. He built what God told him to build. He walked through the door when God told him to walk through it. And God shut the door behind him. Salvation was secure not because Noah was strong, but because God was faithful. Truth steadies me more than I can explain.

Because I don't have the strength to fix the world, but I can walk faithfully within it. I can build what He places in front of me. I can choose obedience in a generation that often shrugs at it. I can trust that redemption still stands, even when wickedness feels loud. Maybe that's the real calling for a simple man in a complicated world — not to solve everything or shout louder than the chaos, but to live faithfully inside the ark of grace. To breathe. To remember. To trust. And to let the light of Christ reflect, however imperfectly, through an ordinary life. Because when darkness surrounds, grace remains. And that changes everything.

Following the Star

Before we talk about eternity, before we wrestle with heaven and hell and what waits beyond the grave, let me tell you about something that happened in a classroom full of third through fifth graders. Last night, my brother in Christ and I were doing our weekly teaching at church, and we found ourselves in Matthew 2 — the story of the Magi. Now, I've read that passage more times than I can count. Most of us have. We picture nativity scenes and Christmas cards, three men in elaborate robes standing near a manger like decorative pieces in a holiday tradition. But teaching children has a way of slowing a story down, and when you slow Scripture down, it has a way of speaking.

The Magi weren't props in a Christmas play. They were seekers. Men from the East, scholars and observers, students of the skies and ancient writings. They saw a star, and instead of dismissing it, they followed it. That alone carries weight. They left what was familiar. Left comfort. Left certainty. All to pursue a sign pointing to a King they had never met. That sounds like faith. The Christian walk often calls us to do the same — to move before every answer is in place, to step forward guided by light we don't yet fully understand.

When the Magi reached Jerusalem, their question stirred the entire city: "Where is He who has been born King of the Jews?" That question unsettled Herod, shook the religious leaders, and forced people to reckon with something bigger than themselves. Truth has a habit of doing that. But what grips me most is what happened when they finally found Him.

There was no palace, no throne, no army — just a child. Humble. Small. Ordinary by the world's standards. And yet, they worshiped, not because of outward appearances, but because of what they recognized in their hearts. Gold. Frankincense. Myrrh. Gifts fit for a King. Glory wrapped in humility. Power revealed through vulnerability. The Gospel has always carried that pattern.

Matthew tells us they returned home in another way, and that feels like more than a travel detail. That's a transformation of language. You don't encounter Christ and leave unchanged. You may still have questions. You may not grasp every mystery. But something shifts. Perspective adjusts. Priorities realign. The Magi went back East, different men than the ones who began the journey, and I can't help but imagine they told the story everywhere they went. "We followed a star." "We found a King." "We worshiped Him." Just like that, the message of Jesus was already stretching beyond Israel's borders before He could even speak.

Standing there in that classroom, watching those kids listen wide-eyed and leaning into the story, something settled into my own heart. Every one of us is following something. A star. An ambition. A relationship. A fear. Something is always guiding our steps. The Magi chose to follow light, and light led them to the Savior. So, the question isn't whether we're following. The question is what. Their story becomes a mirror, gently asking whether we are willing to leave what is comfortable, willing to seek even when it costs something, willing to worship when God shows up in ways we didn't expect.

Because sometimes He doesn't look like a throne. Sometimes He looks like humility. Sometimes He looks like surrender. Sometimes He looks like a child in a manger. The beauty of that classroom moment was that the lesson plan ended, but the Word kept teaching.

It reminded me that following Jesus isn't about having every detail mapped out. It's about taking the next step toward the light He gives. And when you do, you won't return the same way you came. In a world crowded with confusion, doubt, and noise, the star still shines, and it still leads to the Savior. The only question left is whether we are willing to follow it.

Jim Williams

"Your past may explain you—

but it doesn't define you."

— Jim Williams

On Heaven, Hell, and the Gamble of Eternity

Before we ask what happens after death, before we sit with grief and reunion and all those unanswered questions that tend to linger in quiet moments, we must talk about something most folks would rather sidestep: heaven and hell. I'm a simple man — not a scholar, not a philosopher — just someone who carries people in his heart and tries to make sense of the world as I experience it. And here's what I've noticed over the years: you can't really talk about heaven for very long without eventually brushing up against hell. You can't celebrate justice without admitting judgment. You can't speak about good unless evil is real.

People argue about heaven and hell, especially people who say they don't believe in them. Yet even those who reject the words still wrestle with the ideas. Nobody shrugs at injustice and says, "Oh well." Nobody looks at horrific evil and honestly believes it doesn't matter. Something deep inside us cries out. Across cultures, across centuries, across continents, human beings have always sensed there is more. Different names, different imagery, different descriptions — but the same instinctive pull toward meaning. Good should be rewarded. Evil should be answered. That longing doesn't feel accidental to a simple mind like mine.

When I think about it plainly, it lands like this: if there is no heaven, then love, sacrifice, and faithfulness ultimately end in the same dust as cruelty and hatred. If there is no hell, no final reckoning, then evil simply fades without ever being fully answered. And something inside the human heart resists that conclusion. We don't cry out for justice unless we believe justice exists.

157

We don't declare something "wrong" unless right and wrong are more than shifting opinions. The very language we use about fairness, meaning, and accountability sounds strangely eternity-shaped, whether we acknowledge it or not.

I'll be honest about where I stand. I believe the Bible — not because it's convenient or culturally easy, but because it speaks with authority about things my heart already senses. Jesus didn't whisper about eternity; He spoke clearly about life everlasting and judgment. Not to frighten people into compliance, but to tell the truth. Even before faith enters the conversation, human history itself tells an interesting story. Civilizations rise and fall, yet people continue to speak of legacy, meaning, justice, and consequence. They insist some things should never escape accountability. Those are not small thoughts. Those are weighty, beyond-this-life kinds of reflections.

So, here's the question that keeps circling in my mind: if humanity has always sensed something beyond this life, why do so many today dismiss it so quickly? It feels like a dangerous gamble to brush off heaven, to ignore hell, to assume nothing waits beyond the grave — especially when the human heart has whispered otherwise since the beginning. Maybe heaven isn't wishful thinking but fulfillment. Maybe hell isn't cruelty but consequence. Maybe both exist because love is real. After all, choice is real because justice is real. And real things matter.

I don't say any of this with a raised voice. I say it with concern, because eternity isn't merely a doctrine to debate — it's a destination. Pretending it doesn't exist doesn't make it disappear. It only postpones the conversation.

And that's why, before we talk about reunions, before we talk about grief and hope, we have to face the harder question: what truly happens after death? However, we answer that, it inevitably shapes how we live right now.

"I can do all things through him…"

— Philippians 4:13 (ESV)

What Happens After Death?

Before we talk about depression, before we wrestle with the darkest edges of despair, there's another porch conversation that must come first, because what we believe about death shapes how we walk through life. This is one of those slow subjects — the kind you don't rush, the kind where the coffee goes cold because your eyes drift past the yard and into places memory likes to wander. Linnie and I talk about this often. It's been seven years since she lost her mom, and some days it still feels like yesterday. Grief doesn't run on a clock or check a calendar. It simply shows up when it wants to and sits down, whether you invite it or not.

Sometimes our conversations wander toward the reunion. What will it be like? Will she recognize her mama the moment she sees her? Will tears come first, or will joy swallow them whole? Are our loved ones resting now, waiting, or fully awake in glory? Scripture gives glimpses but not blueprints. Paul wrote that to be absent from the body is to be present with the Lord, and that tells this simple man something steady — when a believer closes their eyes here, they open them there. Jesus told the thief on the cross, "Today you will be with Me in paradise." Today. Not centuries from now. Not a long sleep in the dark. Presence. Yet Scripture also points to more still to come — resurrection, glorified bodies, a new heaven and a new earth where death itself is undone. That's a lot for one human mind to hold.

Then, as it often does, the conversation shifts. Linnie has children who don't believe, children who right now don't even want to talk about Jesus. The door closes before the conversation begins.

And that's where things get quiet. Revelation tells us there will be no more tears, no more pain, no sorrow. But how does that work? How can there be perfect peace if someone you love rejects Christ? Will we miss them? Will we remember? Will heaven feel complete? Jesus' story of the rich man and Lazarus reminds us that eternity is conscious, real, and weighty. The rich man remembered. He cared. That passage doesn't answer every question, but it presses the reality of eternity into the conversation.

And this is where I must stop pretending, I can diagram it all. God's Word is clear about the great and steady truths: there is comfort for the believer, there is judgment, there is resurrection, and there is eternity. But the emotional mechanics of how God wipes every tear, how His justice and mercy harmonize in ways we cannot yet fully grasp — that's above my pay grade. My mind is finite. He is not. So, here's what I cling to as a simple man: God is just, and God is good, at the same time, fully and without contradiction. If there is sorrow, He will resolve it. If there is confusion, He will clarify it. If there is heartbreak, He will heal it. And somehow, when we stand in His presence, His judgments will not feel cruel — they will feel right.

Until then, this conversation matters. It makes a husband pray harder. It makes everyday moments feel heavier in the best possible way. Because while we don't understand everything about the next life, we do know this one counts. Every conversation, every prayer, every gentle nudge toward truth, every act of love. If you find yourself thinking about reunions, about loss, about loved ones who don't yet believe, pull up a chair and let it weigh on you. Let it move you toward prayer instead of panic. Let it stir urgency without stealing hope. Some answers will come later. But faith — faith lives right now.

On Suicide, Depression, and a Just Judge

Now this is one of those porch conversations — the kind where the swing slows down, and the coffee cools because neither one of you is in a hurry to speak first. Linnie and I have sat in that kind of quiet more than once, because this subject doesn't tie up neatly. It doesn't end with a verse and a bow. It sits heavily. I live with depression. That's not drama or headlines, just a fact of my life. There have been seasons where the darkness pressed in so tightly, I could barely think straight, seasons where a thought slipped in quietly: *What if I just wasn't here anymore?* Not because I didn't love God. Not because I hated life. But because I was tired — tired of fighting my own mind, tired of carrying weight no one else could see. Sometimes depression isn't a desire to die; it's a desperate desire for relief.

Even in my lowest moments, though, there were anchors that held me steady. My son Austin is one of them. I want to see him graduate. I want to watch him stand at an altar someday. I want to hold his children and tell them stories about their dad. I don't want to miss that life. And then there's Linnie. We haven't had a lifetime together, but I want every day we're given — every laugh, every disagreement, every quiet evening when the house finally settles.

Her kids, my inherited kids, grandbabies running through the house — that kind of noise is holy. It anchors a man. Because I understand depression, I also understand how someone can get so far down that they stop thinking clearly. Linnie sees it differently, and that's okay. She grew up believing suicide was a one-way door, no appeal, no grace. She points to Judas, and she's not wrong to bring him into the conversation.

Scripture is clear about his tragic end. It's also clear that his story carries layers — betrayal, despair, remorse without repentance. But here's where I wrestle as a simple man. I'm not convinced Judas serves as a template for every situation. When someone is buried under clinical depression, when brain chemistry misfires, when trauma stacks year after year and hopelessness clouds judgment, I don't see a clean theological decision being made. I see someone drowning. And when a drowning man thrashes, we don't accuse him of rebellion — we recognize panic. Scripture repeatedly reminds us that Jesus looks at the heart. The unforgivable sin is described as a willful, hardened rejection of the Holy Spirit's saving work.

That's not weakness; that's defiance. Is suicide automatically that? The Bible never says so. What it does show us is that faithful servants of God have known deep despair. Elijah asked God to take his life. Jonah asked to die. Solomon wrote about hating life. Paul admitted he despaired of life itself. These weren't pagans shaking their fists at heaven. These were men crushed under an unbearable weight. And God did not thunder condemnation — He met them in the dark.

That truth matters deeply to me. I believe suicide is a sin because life belongs to God, and our days are ultimately His. But I do not believe suicide outruns the blood of Christ. If one act committed in a moment of mental collapse could cancel saving grace, then grace would be fragile — and my God is not fragile. Salvation rests on Christ's finished work, not on whether I managed to die at my spiritual best. This is not permission, nor is it minimizing the seriousness of such a decision.

It is simply an acknowledgment we must hold carefully: God is perfectly just and perfectly merciful. He knows what rebellion is. He knows what brokenness is. He knows what defiant rejection is, and what is the collapse beneath unbearable pain.

When Linnie and I talk about this, we're not arguing to win. She carries a reverence for holiness and a sense of accountability. I carry compassion for the wounded mind. Somewhere in the middle stands a God who is both Judge and Healer.

If you're reading this from a dark place, if your thoughts have been circling dangerous ground, I want you to hear something steady from this simple man on the porch: you are not weak, you are not faithless, and you are not beyond grace. Depression lies. It tells you you're alone. It tells you you're a burden. It tells you the world would move on just fine without you. It is wrong. Sit here on this porch for a minute. Call someone. Talk to someone. Let someone help carry the weight. There is more life ahead than you can see right now. Sometimes all a soul needs is someone to believe that for them until they can believe it again themselves. You do not have to face the dark alone — and you are worth staying for.

"Strength doesn't come from having it all together—

it comes from knowing where to lean."

— Jim Williams

Dinosaurs, Dragons, and the Bigger Question

Now, before you think this porch swing has gone completely off the rails, stay with me. Sometimes when we talk about faith, freedom, culture, and standing firm, the mind needs a little room to wander. Mine did the other day, and wouldn't you know it, it wandered straight into dinosaurs. That usually happens when my brain refuses to sit still and starts poking at the kinds of questions folks say are unnecessary. "Why does that matter?" "Why even go there?" I don't always have a polished answer for that. I just know curiosity has always been part of how I love God.

So, I did what I tend to do when questions start rattling around in my head — I started digging. The word dinosaur itself didn't appear until the 1800s, which means Moses wasn't writing about a T-Rex by name. But that doesn't mean the Bible is silent about massive, awe-inspiring creatures. That's where things started getting interesting. In the Old Testament, there's a Hebrew word, tannin, which, depending on the translation, is rendered as dragon, serpent, or sea monster. It shows up nearly thirty times. Sometimes connected to the water, sometimes described on land. Whatever those writers were referencing, it certainly doesn't read like something you'd keep in a glass tank on your kitchen counter.

Then there's the behemoth described in Job 40. God points Job to this creature, almost like a father showing his son something magnificent, saying, "Look at this. I made this." Bones are like bronze. Limbs like iron. A tail compared to a cedar tree. Now I've seen hippos. I've seen elephants.

Their tails don't exactly bring cedar trees to mind. That description feels... bigger. Right behind that comes Leviathan in Job 41, a creature portrayed as so fearsome that weapons are useless against it, courage melts before it, and God Himself declares that nothing on earth is its equal. That doesn't read like a casual metaphor. It reads like something that inspired real awe, maybe even real fear.

Now I'll say this plainly — good and faithful scholars disagree on what these creatures represent. Some see poetic imagery. Some see symbolic language. Some see known animals described through an ancient lens. Others allow room for extinct species we can't fully categorize today. Scripture deserves careful handling, not sensational conclusions. But curiosity still lingers. In the documentary *Is Genesis History?*, researchers discuss soft tissue discovered in dinosaur fossils — blood vessels, collagen structures. That doesn't automatically overturn long-held scientific timelines, but it does raise questions about preservation, assumptions, and how we interpret physical evidence.

Add to that the fact that nearly every ancient civilization left behind stories and artwork depicting massive reptilian creatures. From China to Europe to the Americas, dragons appear in carvings, pottery, mosaics, and folklore. Marco Polo even wrote of enormous serpents with claws and jaws wide enough to swallow a man. They didn't use the word dinosaur, but they clearly believed something large and reptilian once roamed the earth. So, are dinosaurs in the Bible? The honest answer is it depends on how you read it. Young-earth believers see no problem with dinosaurs and humans sharing a timeline. Old-earth believers see dinosaurs as long extinct before Adam ever walked the garden. Both groups love Jesus. Both take Scripture seriously. They simply interpret the data differently.

And here's where the simple man in me finally settles down. The Bible doesn't need dinosaurs to prove itself, and it doesn't crumble if they existed alongside man. The Bible is not primarily a science textbook — it's a redemption story. From Genesis to Revelation, it points to Jesus. That's the center. If dinosaurs lived millions of years ago, God made them. If they walked beside Adam, roamed after the Flood, or were remembered in ancient stories, God made them. Either way, the Creator doesn't shrink. If anything, He grows larger in my mind. Creation declares His glory, whether it's a sparrow hopping across your yard or a creature so massive that the ground trembles beneath its feet.

Maybe we argue so fiercely about timelines because we're afraid something might unravel. But truth doesn't unravel under honest questions, and faith isn't nearly as fragile as we sometimes imagine. Maybe the better question isn't, "Are dinosaurs in the Bible?" Maybe it's, "What does creation — seen and unseen — tell us about the Creator?" Whether it's a dragon in Job, a fossil in a museum, or a child staring wide-eyed at a skeleton the size of a bus, all of it whispers the same steady truth: there is Someone bigger than us, stronger than us, smarter than us, and wonderfully creative. And if He can design something that powerful, then maybe — just maybe — He can handle the complexities of my life too. Now that's a porch conversation worth having.

"The Lord will fight for you…"

— Exodus 14:14 (ESV)

Sparks of Growth

Ferris Bueller's Day Off gave us a line that's always stuck with me:

"Life moves pretty fast. If you don't stop and look around once in a while, you could miss it."

The older I get, the more I realize that it's not just a clever movie quote — it's truth.

Life has handed me sparks. Some loud. Some quiet. Some that felt like fireworks. Others like a single coal glowing steadily in the dark. Every one of them shaped me. Every one of them taught me something about growth, about God, about family, about love.

And when I slow down long enough to look around, I see the thread that ties them all together.

"Not every battle is yours to win—

some are yours to trust."

— Jim Williams

Campfires with Austin

You know, I can still remember the first day Austin put on his blue Tiger Cub Scout uniform. Man, I was proud—proud in a way that hits you right here in your chest. Scouting had been a big part of my own childhood, and I always wished I'd had my dad there with me. So, when Austin got that uniform on, I thought, "This is my chance. I can just be his dad and watch him grow."

Well… that didn't last long. Our pack was floundering, and before I knew it, the unit rep asked me to step in as a leader. Suddenly, I wasn't just his dad; I was helping guide the whole program. It's a little intimidating, yeah—but also kind of cool. We've got to build something together.

But let me tell you, this isn't really about me. It's about Austin and the adventures we shared. We camped on the USS Yorktown, bundled up in a tiny one-man tent at winter camp just to stay warm—I can still feel that cold biting through the fabric and his little hand curled up in mine, trying to share what warmth we could. And there were campfires—oh, the campfires. The smell of wood smoke, the quiet crackle, the stories we'd tell each other as the sky turned from pink to deep navy.

I remember one night, him poking at the embers and asking, "Dad, do you think I can do all this on my own someday?" And I told him, "I don't just think you can, Austin. I know you can. And I'll be here if you need me." Those are the moments that stick.

Then came Webelos. That's when he started stretching out a little, doing things on his own while I stayed nearby. A safety net. And I'll tell you, watching that happen is… different. You're proud, sure, but it's also a little scary. Then came the Arrow of Light and the big crossover. That blue-and-gold uniform got tucked away, and now it was khaki and green. Merit badges, summer camps at Camp Barnhardt, new responsibilities… and me, just standing back, arms folded, watching my son grow into a young man. It's a strange feeling. Pride mixed with awe.

Scouting… It's a lot like life, isn't it? At first, the leader carries the weight, shows the way. Then, with guidance, independence grows. And eventually, they're on their own, facing challenges and triumphs with what they've learned. I remember one night, lying in the hammock with him, the stars overhead, him whispering, "Dad… thanks for everything." And I said, "You don't need to thank me, son. Just live it well, that's enough." Simple, small moments—but they stick with you.

One of my proudest moments? When he was tapped for the Order of the Arrow. That's a big deal in scouting—only for those who live the ideals. I'd been a member myself, so being there during his ordeal… I'll never forget it. He pushed through. He made it. He earned his way to Life Scout before his interests shifted elsewhere. But those campfire nights, those talks in hammocks, the long drives, the laughter—they stay with you.

It's funny how life works. You guide them, you teach, you love… and then you step back, just watch them fly. And if you do it right, they'll carry what you've shared with them for a lifetime. That's what I see every time I look at Austin. And I wouldn't trade a second of it.

My Heir, My Namesake

Let me tell you about my boy. While the world was mourning the death of Pope John Paul II, our little man was getting ready to make his entrance. The news stations were somber. Flags were lowered. Commentators spoke in careful tones about history turning a page. And in a hospital room somewhere, another story was quietly beginning.

Austin was six weeks early. I guess he couldn't wait for anybody. Though if you ask me, he timed it just right. He waited until all his grandparents had made it into town before he decided to show up. Around two in the morning, his mama went into labor, and by four that afternoon, he made his debut. She had been laboring all day. I'm sure by that point, excitement was mixed with exhaustion. But when he arrived, none of that mattered. He was early, yes. A little jaundice. But strong. Healthy. Loud enough to let the world know he was here.

And just like that, I wasn't just a man anymore. I was a dad.

Austin is my son. My heir. Our namesake. The one who carries the family line forward. There's something about that as a father — knowing your name, your story, your lessons — they don't end with you. They move forward through him. That realization settles deep in a man's bones.

But I'll tell you something else. He grew up fast.

One day, he was wobbling across the living room floor, talking in half-words. Next, he was standing at the door with a backpack on, heading to his first day of school.

We got him into Cub Scouts, and that started an adventure for both of us. Campouts. Pinewood Derby cars. Merit badges. He worked his way up to Life Scout, and that's nothing to shrug at. I was proud of him.

Around that time, I was working in NASCAR, and he got to travel with me. He saw racetracks, different states, and different experiences. Truth be told, he saw more of the world at his age than I ever did at mine. Those were good days — loud, fast, full.

Then middle school hit, and he told me he wanted to join the band. I remember thinking, "Well… we'll see how long this lasts." He started with the clarinet. Scouts slowly took a back seat, and music took the wheel — and it never let go. High school band became a passion. Marching. Practicing. Competitions. Long nights and early mornings.

Now I've got a Catamount son at Western Carolina University. He's in the band there — Pride of the Mountains. Majoring in music education. He doesn't just want to perform; he wants to teach other kids how to play. That humbles me. There's something steady about a young man who wants to pour into others.

Now, don't think it's been all smooth.

One afternoon, he was out riding his bike while I was inside the house. My phone buzzed. A text from him: "Dad, I fell. I think I broke my leg." I ran outside and found him on the ground. I said what most dads probably say at first.

"Get up. You're fine." I reached down to help him up — and I saw it shift. I made a sound I can't even spell. His femur was broken.

They put a rod in his leg. Surgery. Recovery. Pain. But he was a trooper. Tougher than I realized. And somehow, that break didn't break his spirit. It didn't stop him from marching.

Then came a different kind of break. His mom and I divorced. That hurt him. I know it did. And knowing that it hurt him hurt me even more. There was tension about the season. Some distance. Some silence. But I understood. He didn't want sides. He wanted his whole family. And I can't blame him for that.

Time has a way of standing down rough edges. Today we're close. We talked. We laugh. We've rebuilt what tension once tried to strain. And I couldn't be prouder of the man he's becoming.

I look forward to the day he stands at an altar. I look forward to watching him become a husband, a father. I even look forward — Lord willing — to officiating his wedding myself.

From a six-weeks-early little boy entering a mourning world… to a young man leading music and shaping the next generation.

That's my son. My heir. My namesake.

And if being a father has taught me anything, it's this: you blink… and they're grown.

So, hold the small hands while you can.

One day, they'll be steadying yours.

"Wait for the Lord;

be strong, and let your heart take courage…"

— Psalm 27:14 (ESV)

A Seat at the Table

As a simple man in a complicated world, I've learned something about family. Blood matters. But love matters more.

Austin made me a dad the day he was born. That's my boy. Always will be. There's something sacred about that bond—the first cry, the first steps, the first time he called me "Dad." Don't forget those moments. They mark you. They change you. They root themselves deep in your heart in a way only a parent understands.

But fatherhood doesn't stop at biology.

Katelyn was twenty-one when her mom and I met. She wasn't a little girl needing bedtime stories or someone to chase monsters out from under the bed. She was already stepping into adulthood. Forming her own opinions. Carrying her own wounds. Trying to make sense of her own story and her place in it.

Now she's twenty-eight.

And somewhere over these years, she stopped being "Linnie's daughter" and just became... mine.

Her biological father hasn't really been present. And that kind of absence doesn't just disappear because you turn eighteen. It doesn't fade away when you get your own apartment or pay your own bills. It settles quietly in the background. It shapes identity. It raises silent questions you may never say out loud: Am I wanted? Do I belong? Who claims me?

So, one day, I asked her something that had been sitting on my heart for a while. I said, "Would you let me adopt you?" Even as an adult.

And she said yes.

We'll be heading to the courthouse soon. No big production. No dramatic music playing in the background. Just paperwork. Signatures. A judge. A simple legal act.

But what it represents is far bigger than ink on a page.

It says you're not temporary. You're not tolerated. You're chosen.

At twenty-eight, she doesn't "need" a dad the way a five-year-old does. But here's something I've come to understand—you never outgrow the need to belong. You never outgrow the quiet comfort of knowing someone claims you without hesitation.

And the more I think about it, the more I see God in it.

Romans 8:15 says we have received the Spirit of adoption, by whom we cry, "Abba, Father." Adoption. That word isn't accidental. God didn't just rescue us from sin and leave us standing at the edge of heaven like distant relatives. He brought us into the family. He gave us His name. He made us heirs.

Ephesians 1:5 says He predestined us for adoption through Jesus Christ. Think about that. Before we cleaned ourselves up. Before we ever understood doctrine. Before we ever "got it right." He chose us.

That courthouse trip for Katelyn? That's my small, human reflection of a much bigger spiritual truth.

I can't rewrite her past. I can't erase wounds. I can't answer every question she has about faith, suffering, or why certain things happened the way they did. But I can stand before a judge and make something official that my heart has decided a long time ago.

You're mine.

And if a flawed man like me can look at a grown woman and say, "I want you to carry my name," how much more does a perfect Father look at us and say the same?

Family isn't always about blood. Sometimes it's about grace. Sometimes it's about choosing someone and not letting go.

And sometimes the most powerful words a father can say whether to a child of five or twenty-eight—are simply this:

You belong.

"Waiting isn't wasted—

it's preparation."

— Jim Williams

Loving Kids Who Don't Share Your Name

Children are a blessing. And children are hard. Biological kids are hard enough. You're learning on the fly, praying you don't mess them up too badly, trying to love them and lead them at the same time. Stepchildren? That's a whole different animal. There's defiance. There's pushing limits. There's that classic line: "You're not my dad. You can't tell me what to do." And then there's the tension of discipline, the unspoken question of how far is too far, the fear of overstepping, the awkward dance between loving them and leading them. I know some of you sitting on this porch can nod along. It's hard, isn't it?

When I married Linnie, her two boys were already in the house. Good boys. Smart boys. Good-looking boys. Full of potential. And I'll be honest about something that mattered more to me than I expected—I wanted us to be a family. Not by forcing anything. Not by making them take my name. Their last name was Lewis, and I respected that. But in my own simple way, I wanted something that symbolized us. So, for fun, we combined our names—Williams and Lewis. Willewis. It was lighthearted and playful, but underneath it was something real. A quiet hope that we weren't just people sharing a house; we were building something together. A family isn't just paperwork. It's belonging.

Now back to reality. When their mom and I would sit them down to talk, sometimes it felt like we'd get more response from the drywall. They were convinced they knew better.

And if I'm honest, I saw a lot of myself in that. We had rough patches. Raised voices. Hard conversations. Long silences. I often saw myself as the drill instructor. Recruits don't like boot camp. They don't clap for the guy making them do push-ups. But when they hit the real world, they understand why the training mattered. Maybe I leaned too hard sometimes. But my heart was simple—I wanted better for them. I wanted them to avoid some of the potholes their mom and I had stepped into. I wanted them to veer away from some of the pain we knew too well.

Proverbs 22:6 says, "Train up a child in the way he should go; even when he is old, he will not depart from it." It doesn't say they won't argue about it. It doesn't say they won't resist it. It just says the training sticks. They're seven or eight years older now than when I first met them. They've grown. Matured. Made decisions—some good, some learning experiences. They didn't take all my advice. Usually it's after the hard lesson, after the mistake, after the consequence that I hear, "Yeah… you were right." Funny how that works.

But isn't that exactly how we are with God? He tells us which road leads to life. We nod… then grab the wheel ourselves. We think we know better. We test limits. We learn the hard way. And somewhere down the road we whisper, "You were right." Hebrews 12 talks about how a father disciplines the child he loves—not to harm, not to control, but to shape, to protect, to prepare. As earthly parents—biological or step—we're trying to reflect that. Imperfection, yes. But intentionally.

There's another tension too: helping versus enabling. Whatever they go through, we'll be there. Not to rescue them from every consequence. Not to shield them from every storm. But to help. Truly help. That's love. And I think that's how God sees us.

He doesn't disown us when we push back. He doesn't walk away when we say, "You can't tell me what to do." He stays. He corrects. He waits. He welcomes us back when we finally circle around.

Step-parenting has taught me something deep: love isn't always soft. Sometimes love is steady. Sometimes love is firm. Sometimes love is saying the hard thing and risking being misunderstood. And sometimes, years later, when the noise settles, you realize the seeds were taking root the whole time. Raising kids—any kids— isn't about control. It's about pointing them toward the Lord. Deuteronomy 6 tells us to impress His commandments on them, to talk about them when you sit at home and when you walk along the road. That's not a one-time speech. That's daily living.

So, to the stepdads and stepmoms out there who feel like outsiders in their own house some days—stay steady. Keep loving. Keep training. Even when they roll their eyes. Even when they think they know better. Because one day, they just might look back and realize you weren't the enemy. You were preparing them for life. And maybe—just maybe—you were reflecting a Father who never stopped doing the same for you.

And as for that silly little name we made up—Willewis—funny thing is, over time, it stopped feeling silly. Because somewhere between the arguments, the eyerolls, the hard talk, and the growing pains, we really did become a family. Not because of a last name, but because love stayed. And if you'll allow me one last front-porch thought before you head back inside, family isn't built in the easy moments. It's built in the staying.

"The heart of man plans his way,

but the Lord establishes his steps."

— Proverbs 16:9 (ESV)

Life is a Team Sport

It was during my time at Hendrick Motorsports that I first heard a phrase that has stayed with me ever since: "Life is a team sport." It wasn't written in a book or delivered in a sermon. It was something we wore—literally—on blue rubber bracelets, a daily reminder of how things really worked in that environment. At the time, I understood it in a practical sense. Racing is built on teamwork. But looking back now, I realize it was teaching me something far deeper than I knew at that moment.

During those years, I had a front row seat to what most people only ever see from a distance. We were one of the most dominant teams in NASCAR, winning races and championships, operating at a level that demanded excellence in every detail. I worked around drivers like Jimmie Johnson, Jeff Gordon, Dale Earnhardt Jr., Kyle Busch, Mark Martin, and Casey Mears, names that carry weight in the sport. From the outside, it is easy to believe those men carried the success on their own. But being inside that world showed me a different truth. They didn't do it alone. They couldn't.

What people often miss is everything that happens behind the scenes. The pit crew is moving with precision. Engineers are making decisions that most people will never understand. The mechanics are working long hours without recognition. The ones turning wrenches, analyzing data, preparing cars, and solving problems before anyone else even knows they exist. Without them, the driver is just a man in a car. Talent matters, but without the right team, even the most gifted individual cannot win.

Leadership played a role in that as well. Mr. Hendrick didn't just expect results; he expected effort. He expected accountability. But what stood out most was how he valued people. Not just the ones in the spotlight, but everyone. The man cutting the grass mattered. The person sweeping the shop floor mattered.

There was an understanding that every role, no matter how small it seemed, contributed to something bigger. That kind of leadership builds more than success; it builds culture.

As I've walked further in my faith, I've come to see how closely that mirrors what Scripture teaches about the Church. In 1 Corinthians 12:12, Paul writes, "For just as the body is one and has many members, and all the members of the body, though many, are one body…" That truth carries weight. Different people, different gifts, different roles—but one body. And just like in racing, when one part isn't functioning as it should, it affects everything.

Somewhere along the way, many of us began to believe that we are supposed to do life on our own. That we should figure it out ourselves, carry it ourselves, handle it ourselves. But that was never God's design. Ecclesiastes 4:9–10 reminds us, "Two are better than one… For if they fall, one will lift up his fellow." We were created for connection. We were created for community. We were created to walk alongside one another, not apart from one another.

Looking back, that season of my life gave me more than a career experience. It was a place where God began doing a deeper work in me. It was there that I gave my life to Christ. And while I learned a great deal about racing, what stayed with me the most were the lessons about people, about teamwork, about leadership, and about the reality that success is never a solo act. There is always more happening than what can be seen.

Whether you find yourself in the spotlight or behind the scenes, your role matters. The outcome is never built on one person alone. It is built on the collective effort of many, each doing their part with purpose and commitment. That is true in racing, and it is true in life.

From the Porch, the lesson is simple: you were never meant to do this alone. Find your people. Walk with them. Serve alongside them. Because at the end of the day, life is not about what one person can accomplish by themselves—it is about what God can do through a group of people who are willing to work together.

"My plans got me here—

but God's steps carried me through."

— Jim Williams

Crossing the Pit Wall

This will be a day I will not soon forget. Just a few years before, I was a spectator in the stands, cheering on the drivers and dreaming of what it might be like to be part of the action. Now, I was sitting on the pit wall at Daytona International Speedway—the world center of speed, the mecca of racing.

I was working at Hendrick Motorsports, part of a developmental pit crew. Our crew had been leased out to an ARCA team to get real experience. This was where we cut our teeth, learning the precision, speed, and discipline needed to reach Cup Racing.

It was a crisp February morning. Standing in the garage as the gates opened, there was a strange calm before the storm. Engines roared to life, crews ran through last-minute checks, and the air smelled of fuel, rubber, and the weather adhesive used to glue lug nuts onto rims—that glue made 12-second tire changes possible.

I slipped into my three-layer fire suit, fireproof shoes, helmet, and gloves, then walked out to pit road and sat on the wall, just taking it all in. My eyes drifted to the letters along the wall spelling "DAYTONA." I thought, I'm here. This is it.

The final preparations were underway: the pit stall was set; the road crew pushed the car to the starting grid. We all lined up on pit road as the national anthem played over the loudspeaker.

The flag flapped in the Daytona breeze, and a flyover by elite military pilots capped off the moment. Then the engines fired, the race came alive, and it was time to work.

A fuel can—one of those 11-gallon beasts weighing about 60 pounds—was handed to me and hoisted onto my shoulder. I looked down pit road as the car approached, listening to the spotter call out the stalls. My adrenaline was pumping. The jackman, tire changers, and carriers moved into position.

As the car came to a stop, I instantly stood and plugged the fuel can into the car. This stop would take both cans. As I stepped back and tossed the empty can across the wall into a teammate's hands, the second can was handed to me. The tire changers and carriers moved to the other side. The car went up, all four tires off the ground, and I plugged in the second tank. I watched my catch-can guy for the nod that the tank was full. The car went down, tires on, and I sprinted alongside to maximize the fuel going in. Full.

We returned to our positions, ready for the next stop, the next dance. That was my first pit stop in the big leagues, and I'll never forget the rush, the smell, the sounds, and the pure adrenaline of being part of it.

The First Win

Well, there are a lot of "first wins" in racing, depending on how you define them. My first win on a NASCAR team was with Kyle Busch in the #5 Lowe's Busch Series car—but I wasn't at the track. I didn't experience the chaos, the smells, or the adrenaline firsthand.

My first race win as a crew member at the Cup level—that was something else entirely. I wasn't the gasman, but I was part of the fueling crew. I was the guy catching the second can, then carting the tanks back to the Sunoco fuel pumps, filling them, and bringing them back to the pit box to weigh them. See, we don't have fuel gauges in the car, so we measure by the pound to know exactly how much gas we're using.

This particular race was the Coke 600, the longest race of the year - 600 miles of speed, strategy, and stamina. I was on the #25 National Guard / GMAC car, driven by Casey Mears. That year, we had a special digital camo paint scheme to represent the National Guard, and it was Memorial Day weekend—so not only was it the longest race, but it also had extra meaning and honor behind it.

We ran a smart race. The Coke 600 often turns into a fuel-mileage battle, and that worked in our favor. Cars began dropping out as they ran dry. Slowly, lap by lap, we found ourselves moving up. And then, suddenly, we were leading. My heart was racing. Could this be it? Could this be the "W"?

Casey had never won a Cup race before, and the #25 car hadn't seen victory in years. That final lap felt like it lasted forever, but only the last lap mattered. And we did it. We crossed the finish line first. The pit crew erupted—pumping fists, high-fiving, laughing, shouting. The radio crackled to life, and I'll never forget Casey's words: "I'm out of gas."

It didn't matter. That win was ours. That night, we all shared a moment that only comes along once in a lifetime, a combination of preparation, teamwork, timing, and a little bit of luck. Being part of that win, knowing the role I played in the background, was exhilarating. It was the kind of first win that cement a memory, one you carry with you forever.

Full-Page in the Paper

The next year, 2008, things had shifted. I was still with Hendrick Motorsports, but the #25 car was gone, replaced by the #88. Hendrick had just hired one of the biggest names in NASCAR — Dale Earnhardt Jr. Excitement was everywhere. Suddenly, we weren't just crew members; we were crew members for one of the most popular drivers in the sport. The energy around the garage felt different — charged, electric. You could sense it in conversations, in expectations, in that quiet understanding that something big was unfolding right in front of us.

Then, out of the blue, I got a call from the paper back home. My old friend — a lieutenant in the fire department — had given them my name and number. They wanted to make a story. A full-page story. About me. About my journey. About being on Dale Jr.'s team. I remember standing there holding that phone, a strange mix of disbelief and pride washing over me. One whole page back home. Not for a single win. Not for some flashy headlines. But for the road that led me there — the long nights, the sweat, the learning, the ups, the downs, all the sparks along the way that had carried me further than I ever imagined.

When I finally flipped through that newspaper and saw my picture staring back at me, something settled quietly inside. It wasn't ego. It wasn't loud pride. It was something deeper — perspective. Because that page wasn't really about recognition. It was about the journey. From a kid dreaming in the stands to a man living the dream in the pits.

From watching heroes on television to working alongside them. From wondering if I'd ever truly find my place to realizing I had been walking toward it all along.

In that moment, I understood something life keeps teaching me over and over: these sparks — big or small, quiet or loud — matter more than we sometimes realize. They light the path forward. They remind you why the work matters, why the sacrifices matter, why the hard seasons matter. They remind you that being part of something bigger than yourself is worth every single step. Because sometimes the victory isn't measured in trophies. Sometimes it's measured in moments where you pause, look back, and whisper, "God… I never saw this coming."

Being Let Go

The thrill of victory… and the agony of defeat." Jim McKay used to say those words on *Wide World of Sports*, and when I was younger, they just sounded dramatic, something that belonged to athletes, trophies, and highlight reels. It was a phrase for television. For somebody else's story. But life has a way of taking old phrases and turning them into something personal.

It was the end of the 2009 season. December. I had gotten saved in 2008 and baptized in October of 2009. My life had changed spiritually in ways I was still trying to understand. And now… I was losing my job. I was standing in the shop where I worked, and the hum of the garage felt strangely hollow that day. The tools were where they always were. The cars were where they always sat. Nothing had physically changed. But something in the air felt different.

Then I saw the team manager walk in. Our eyes met, and I felt that familiar knot tighten in my stomach, the kind of knot that doesn't need words. The kind that already knows. He called me over, and I followed him upstairs to his office. Inside were the crew chief and my supervisor. Three men. Three faces. One conversation is waiting to happen. They didn't waste time. They gave me the news plainly. I was being let go. No dramatic music. No slow-motion moment. Just words. Simple. Heavy. Final.

It hit like a kick in the stomach. My chest tightened. My heart pounded. My mind started racing through questions I didn't have answers for. What now? How will this work? What am I supposed to do next? And yet, something unexpected happened in that moment. I lifted my head.

I thanked them for the opportunity to work there. And I said the only thing that felt true: "I believe I was here for a reason… and it's time for me to go."

I told them what that reason was. "I came here. I met Joey. I got saved. I was baptized." And then the words came out before I had fully processed them: "Now God needs me to move on." I could tell they were shocked by my reaction. Honestly, there was a part of me, too. Because if you had looked inside my chest at that moment, you would not have seen confidence. You would have seen fear wrestling with faith.

Still, I shook their hands. I walked out. Head held high. On the outside, I looked composed. Steady. Resolved. But on the inside, I was coming apart. Because faith doesn't erase the sting of loss. Trust doesn't eliminate uncertainty. Peace doesn't mean you don't feel the weight of the moment pressing down on you.

But beneath all the emotion, there was something else. Something steady. Something quiet. Peace. Not because I understood what was coming next. I didn't. Not because I had a backup plan. I didn't have one of those either. The peace came from one simple belief: God wasn't surprised by this. Even if I was.

Even in what felt like defeat, there was purpose. Even in loss, there was movement. Even in agony, there was a spark of growth waiting somewhere ahead. I couldn't see it yet. I couldn't map it out. But I believed it was there. Sometimes the thrill of victory is easy to recognize. The applause. The wins. The promotions. But sometimes the real growth—the deeper work of God—happens in what feels like defeat. In the office upstairs. In the hard conversation. In the moment when the door closes, and you don't know which one will open next. And looking back now, I can say this with conviction: that loss didn't end my story. It redirected it.

Endurance Wears an Apron

That's the thought that keeps coming back to me as we sit here on this warm Carolina summer night. Go ahead and top off your glass, because this one belongs to a remarkable woman — my grandmother.

The older I get, the more I understand who she was and what she carried. She's been gone since 1996, yet her fingerprints remain everywhere in my life. My memories don't begin with childhood scenes of parents standing side by side. My memories begin with her. I called her Mama — and she rightly earned that name. She took me in when I was just 13 months old and raised me as her own. I was her youngest son's boy, born into circumstances I was far too young to understand. My dad was 24. My mom was 17. They weren't together, and whatever storms were blowing back then belonged to a world beyond my awareness. But Mama never spoke bitterness into that story. When questions came, she would simply say, "They were too young." No blame. No resentment. Just grace. That alone tells you something about her character.

It wasn't until I was much older that I began to grasp the depth of her endurance. While piecing together my family tree years later, I stumbled across a detail that made me smile. Mama got married in May. Her first child arrived in July. I remember sitting there thinking, "Well now… math isn't quite mathing," and then laughing quietly to myself. Life has always been messier than the tidy timelines we prefer. Mama's story certainly was. My grandfather — a man I never had the privilege of meeting — was killed in a work accident when my dad was only a year old. Mama was 35 years old, suddenly widowed, with three small children, all under five.

Thirty-five. I can barely wrap my mind around that now. Later, she got married and had one more child, my Aunt Jerrie, who would help raise me alongside Mama. But that second marriage brought hardship instead of ease. He was an alcoholic, prone to disappearing for days and returning with anger in tow. I grew up hearing stories from my dad that once sounded distant but now feel like evidence of Mama's resilience — about nights when he and my Uncle Ray had to step in, pulling him off her and throwing him out of the house.

By the time Mama took me in, she was moving into her 60s. Think about that for a moment. She had already raised her children. They were grown. She had every right to slow down, to rest, to finally breathe without the weight of diapers and discipline and daily sacrifice. Instead, she started over. With me. And never once did I feel like anything other than her child. There was no sense of being a grandson raised by a grandmother. I was hers — fully, completely, without condition. Her name was Gladys, a good old-fashioned country name. The family had a playful nickname for her, one she didn't particularly enjoy being used in public, so naturally, another one took its place: Happy Tail. And truthfully, that suited her spirit far better.

We didn't have much growing up, at least not by the world's measuring stick. But somehow, we always had enough. Enough food. Enough love. Enough laughter. Enough discipline to keep me mostly pointed in the right direction. Mama raised me according to what she believed was right, not according to shifting trends or cultural winds. In many ways, I grew up feeling like I belonged to a generation behind my peers. And I count that as a blessing. She taught me countless lessons, but the one that echoes loudest through my life is this: endure. Stand steady. Keep going.

Life, of course, is filled with other relationships along the way. I saw my dad from time to time.

Years later, he explained in a letter why distance marked much of those early years. There were reasons — complicated, painful, human reasons. My biological mom remains a gentler, quieter chapter. I don't remember her from my earliest days, though I have photographs of her holding me during visits. My memories of her truly begin around the age of ten — trips to South Carolina, summers that felt like grand adventures for a boy who had barely crossed state lines. I still remember the first time I saw that giant peach water tower, standing there in absolute awe. Mama worried during those visits, not from jealousy but from fear — fear born from a lifetime of loss — that my mother might not bring me back. But she always did. Those summers were good ones.

As adulthood arrived, life carried me into new chapters — South Carolina for a season, then back home to eastern North Carolina. We stayed connected, though never woven tightly into daily routines. No bitterness lived there. Just the natural spacing that sometimes forms when lives follow different roads. Later, traveling with a NASCAR show car brought our paths together more often. After that chapter ended, the visits grew fewer. And fewer. And fewer. Now my mother is older. She doesn't drive much. We keep up with each other the modern way — through screens, shared photos, quiet glimpses into each other's lives. I know, like her son, I should visit more often than I do. But hear this plainly: there is no ill will in my heart. Only love.

Life gave me several women who carried the title of "mother" in different ways. But Mama — my grandmother — is the one who first showed me what steady, sacrificial love looks like. The kind of love that starts over when it has every right not to.

The kind of endurance that doesn't make speeches but quietly puts on an apron and gets back to work.

And even now, sitting here on this porch, I can still feel the strength of that woman echoing through my story.

From Victory Lane to the Back of the Bus

Can I get real for a minute? Some days… your job just flat-out stinks. There are mornings you don't feel called—you feel stuck. You think about quitting. You think about walking out. Then you check your bank account and realize… that's not today. I've been there. I've had those mornings where the alarm goes off, and I lie there staring at the ceiling, bargaining with God and my responsibilities at the same time.

I've had some cool jobs in my life. Early on, I was a firefighter. Lights and sirens. Kicking in doors. Helping people on what might've been the worst day of their lives. There's purpose in that. There's adrenaline. There's pride. You feel like you're doing something that matters because everybody can see it matters. Then came NASCAR. Fast cars. Loud engines. Standing in Victory Lane after a win. Being part of something that the whole country watched on Sunday afternoons. I tell folks I've had two great careers.

And then there's this one.

Now I'm a TSA, not airport security. A Transportation Safety Assistant. You know what that means? I ride in the back of a school bus. Every day. We pick up EC kids—Exceptional Children—and Impact students. Some have physical disabilities. Some have learning challenges. Some have behavioral struggles that the world doesn't quite know what to do with. I call them EGR kids. Extra Grace Required.

Not glamorous, huh? Not exactly lights and sirens. Not exactly champagne in Victory Lane. Just a man riding in the back of a bus, making sure everybody stays safe.

And I'll admit, when I first stepped into this role, my pride had to take a seat. It didn't sound impressive.

It didn't carry the same weight when someone asked, "So what do you do?" There are no dramatic stories to tell at parties. No trophies. No applause. Just early mornings, bus seats, and a reflective vest.

But let me tell you something—this has been the most rewarding job I've ever had.

Yes, I've helped pull people out of burning houses. Yes, I've stood in moments most folks only see on TV. But building relationships with kids? Watching trust form slowly? Seeing a child who struggles feel seen? That's different. That hits somewhere deeper.

There's a little boy who barely speaks to anyone—but he'll fist bump me every morning. That's our thing. No words. Just a small connection. There's a young lady who has hard days, and I mean hard days. But she knows I'm steady. I'm there. Same seat. Same smile. Same calm voice. No spotlight. Just presence.

And maybe that's the point.

We live in a world that chases titles and applause. We measure success by how impressive it sounds when we say it out loud. "Firefighter." That gets nods. "NASCAR." That gets stories. "Bus monitor." Not so much.

But here's what I've learned as a simple man in a complicated world: purpose doesn't always wear a uniform people admire. Sometimes it wears a reflective vest and rides in the back of a bus. Sometimes, purpose looks small on paper but huge in eternity.

If you're somewhere right now that feels small… if your job doesn't sound impressive at dinner conversations… if you feel like you took a step down instead of up… I want to tell you something I've had to tell myself.

Be where you are. Be present. Be excellent.

You don't know who's watching you. You don't know which kid sees you as the safest adult in their entire day. You don't know whose life you're steadying just by showing up consistently. Faithfulness isn't flashy. It's repetitive. It's ordinary. It's daily.

It doesn't have to be glamorous. It just has to be faithful.

And sometimes the greatest impact you'll ever make won't happen in Victory Lane.

It'll happen in seat number three on the left.

Jim Williams

"Above all, keep loving one another earnestly…"

— 1 Peter 4:8 (ESV)

Quest — Reconnecting with Dad

That layoff led to Quest. Quest… wow. Where do I even start? I guess right at the beginning.

It was January 2010. I still didn't have a job. The racing industry had let go of a lot of people at the end of the previous year, and opportunities were scarce. Doors weren't exactly flying open. If anything, they felt like they were slamming shut faster than I could knock. I was uncertain about everything — direction, provision, purpose. All of it.

Since I had been saved, I'd been faithfully attending the men's nights at the church I had been invited to. Those nights became an anchor for me, a place where faith felt real, where conversations were honest, where men talked about struggles instead of pretending they didn't have any. That night, they had a special speaker: Nikita Koloff.

For the younger folks reading this, Nikita was "The Russian Nightmare," a WWF wrestler I had watched as a kid. Larger than life. A television character suddenly stood right there in front of me. Meeting him felt surreal, even more so when he signed an old photo I had of him with his uncle Ivan Koloff — his fresh signature sitting beside Ivan's from years before.

But Nikita wasn't there to talk about wrestling. He was there to talk about Quest.

He shared how those five and a half days had changed his life, how it had shaken things loose, how it had impacted him so deeply that he became, for lack of a better word, an ambassador for it. I listened intently, because by then I was hungry for God — hungry for growth, hungry for something deeper than just attending church.

I wanted this. Badly.

There was just one problem: I had no job, which meant I couldn't afford it.

Then Nikita said something I didn't see coming.

"Go home, sign up for the February Quest… and I'll call you tomorrow."

Simple words. Heavy impact.

I did exactly that. The next day, he called. He told me I had a sponsor. The cost was covered. I was on the bus — just like that.

But there was a catch: thirty days of prep work before the event even began. Homework. Reflection. Study. Prayer. Preparation for the journey ahead. At first, it felt daunting. "Man, what did I just sign up for?" But looking back, that prep work became a journey of its own, a slow, quiet stretching of the heart. God was working long before the bus ever left the parking lot.

The night before leaving, Joey handed me a manila envelope.

"Don't open this," he said. "Give it to them before you get on the bus."

No explanation. Just instructions.

So, I did.

The next day, I climbed onto that bus with nineteen other guys, heading to a place I knew nothing about. I didn't know anyone. I didn't know what to expect. I didn't know what was going to happen. I'd be lying if I said I wasn't nervous. Part of me even wondered, "Is there some kind of Kool-Aid ending to this thing?"

What I did know was this: something big was coming.

And it was.

The second night there, I found myself struggling — struggling with thoughts about my mom and dad, wrestling with memories, questions, and emotions I didn't fully understand. Then came that unmistakable nudge, the Holy Spirit pressing gently but persistently.

Forgive them.

I argued in my own head. How do you forgive people for something you never even had? I wasn't angry at them. I didn't grow up with them. How do you miss something you never had? How do you grieve an absence you barely remember?

The nudge didn't stop. It stayed — steady, patient, unrelenting. So finally, I did.

I forgave both my mom and my dad. Not because I suddenly understood everything, but because obedience sometimes comes before clarity.

A few days later, the moment came. The envelope Joey had given me was returned to me. By then, I was already in a vulnerable place — walls lowered, defenses softened, heart exposed.

I opened it.

Inside was a stack of letters from friends and family — words from people who knew me, who loved me, who had walked pieces of life with me. But my eyes went straight to the first letter.

It was from my dad.

He wrote to me. Explained everything — why I had lived with my grandmother, why he hadn't been around, why life unfolded the way it did. Then came the words I never expected to read.

He asked for my forgiveness.

As I sat there reading that letter, something inside me shifted. Years of questions, years of quiet wondering, years of "what-ifs" didn't disappear, but they began to settle. Words on a page brought understanding. Words on a page brought healing.

For the first time, I could see him differently — not just as the dad I never had, but as a man. A flawed man. A human man. A man who had made mistakes, carried regrets, and wished he could rewrite chapters already inked.

Suddenly, grace didn't feel theoretical. It felt personal.

I cried. I forgave him again. And I felt a weight lifted that I didn't even realize I had been carrying.

Quest gave me something I never saw coming — not just a deeper walk with God, but a bridge to my dad. A second chance at a relationship I had quietly assumed was impossible.

That letter didn't fix everything. Life rarely works like that.

It started something — a conversation, a connection, a spark of growth that continues even now.

And sitting here reflecting on it, I can say this with certainty:

God was working in ways far bigger than I could see — long before the bus, long before the envelope, long before I ever understood what He was building.

Loving a Neurodivergent Wife

L ove isn't always what you think it's going to be. Sometimes it's quiet. Sometimes it's messy. Sometimes it's loud. And sometimes it sneaks up on you when you least expect it.

Loving a neurodivergent wife — that's my story. And it has been, without question, the most challenging, the most humbling, and the most rewarding journey of my life.

I met Linnie years after I had started finding my footing in faith and family. By then, life had already taught me a few lessons the hard way. I wasn't the same man I had been in earlier chapters of my story. And then there she was — unlike anyone I had ever known. Bright. Creative. Deeply thoughtful. Intensely focused on the things that mattered most to her. And yes, neurodivergent in ways that sometimes-made life feel like a puzzle I didn't have the right pieces for.

At first, I didn't know how to navigate it. Truthfully, I didn't even fully understand what I was navigating. I had to learn patience in ways I didn't know I needed. I had to listen differently, communicate differently, celebrate differently, and maybe most importantly, learn to love differently.

It wasn't always easy. There were days when communication felt like walking through fog — when what was obvious to her was invisible to me, and what I thought was simple felt overwhelming to her. Moments where misunderstandings weren't about effort or intention, but simply difference. Different wiring. Different processing. Different ways of experiencing the same world.

That's where something important began to shift in me.
I couldn't "fix" her. I couldn't engineer smoother reactions. I couldn't apply some mechanical solutions like tightening a bolt or adjusting timing. All I could do was walk beside her.

And in walking beside her, I found myself being stretched, challenged, refined, and transformed.

Real love has a way of exposing impatience you didn't know you carried, pride you didn't realize was there, and expectations quietly shaping how you measured everything. Somewhere along that journey, we even started a blog together — *Grace in the Gaps* — because we realized something our own life kept teaching us: those gaps, the spaces where misunderstandings live, where patience is tested, where life refuses to follow the neat script we imagined, are where grace either shows up... or everything falls apart.

So, we chose grace.

Over and over.

Not perfectly. Not flawlessly. But intentionally.

Slowly, over time, those gaps stopped feeling like obstacles. They became spaces of growth, understanding, connection — spaces where love deepened instead of fractured.

I remember one night we were sitting together, just talking. No agenda. No plans. No problem to solve. Just the quiet hum of the house around us. And it hit me in a way I hadn't fully grasped before: loving her wasn't about having all the answers. It wasn't about getting everything right. It wasn't about mastering some invisible rulebook. It was about showing up — every day, in big ways and small ways, on easy days and complicated days.

It was about choosing love when it felt simple and choosing love when it felt like work. Choosing patience when I am tired. Choosing understanding when I was frustrated. Choosing grace when misunderstanding would have been easier.

And God, as He so often does, used every bit of it to teach me something deeper.

Love is active. Love is resilient. Love doesn't wait for perfect conditions. Love creates space. Love adjusts. Love endures. Love grows.

Loving Linnie has made me more empathetic, humbler, more patient, and more aware of how differently people experience the same reality. It has made me more dependent on God than I ever expected to be in marriage, and that may be the greatest surprise of all.

I don't have a perfect marriage. I never wanted one. I wanted a real one.

And real marriages, just like real lives, have gaps, struggles, unexpected twists, and moments that stretch you far beyond your comfort zone. But those very places — those uncomfortable spaces, those unplanned challenges — are where life actually happens. They're where God often does His deepest work. They're where growth sparks.

Just like in the pits. At the campfires. In Quest. And in every other unexpected chapter of my life.

Love I've learned, isn't always easy.

But it is always worth it.

Walking this journey with Linnie has shown me that some of life's greatest adventures aren't measured in miles, wins, or accolades. They're measured in grace, patience, understanding, and the quiet, daily courage to love someone fully — not for who you expected them to be, but for who God uniquely created them to be.

"Love isn't always easy—

but it's always worth choosing."

— Jim Williams

He Doesn't Own Her Anymore

Now this next story… most of it isn't mine to tell. What happened in her heart is her testimony. But I can tell you what I saw.

One Sunday afternoon after church, I felt that nudge. Not loud. Not dramatic. Just that steady push that says, Go. Linnie and I love day trips—when the wallet allows it. No real agenda. Just the road and wherever it leads. But that day, I knew where we were headed: Moravian Falls.

I have been there once before. A small waterfall. A quiet place locals call Prayer Mountain. Settled by Moravians in the 1750s—German-speaking believers who, legend says, prayed on that mountain unceasingly for a hundred years. You can't verify every detail of that story. But you can feel something there. There's a stillness. A weight. The sense that prayers have lingered in the air longer than in most places.

We were walking near the falls when we met a couple who said they were missionaries from Indiana, just riding around seeing the sights. If I'm honest… they looked more like bikers than missionaries. Leather. Sunglasses. Road-worn. But God has a habit of wrapping holy moments in unexpected packages.

We started talking. Sharing stories. Swapping testimonies. It was easy. Unforced. Then suddenly the man pulled off his sunglasses, dropped them on the picnic table, and said, "I'm tired of this." It startled us. But he wasn't angry. He just looked burdened. Then he said, "Let's pray."

He began praying over Linnie. And what came out of his mouth wasn't generic. It wasn't surface-level church talk. It was specific. Deep. Like he'd been handed a script to parts of her life no one standing there had told him about.

As he prayed, I noticed she began to sway. I quietly stepped behind her, just in case. And that's when I saw it. Her hands slowly lifted behind her back—like she was standing in handcuffs.

I hadn't said a word about her past.

But the Holy Spirit whispered it clearly in my spirit: bondage.

Before me, Linnie had endured a deeply abusive relationship. The kind that leaves scars you can't see. The kind that plants lie in your identity and let them grow roots. One of those lies had echoed in her for years: "He owns you." That sentence had settled deep in places words don't easily reach.

The missionary's wife saw what I was seeing. She leaned toward her husband and said something quietly. He stopped mid-prayer, looked at me, and said, "You have to pray for her."

So, I stepped forward.

I reached between her hands like I was holding the chain of those invisible cuffs. And I prayed. Not polished. Not rehearsed. Just firm. Just believing. I declared that fear, those scars, that abuse—they go to the foot of the cross. They do not get to control her anymore. In my spirit, I broke the chains.

She collapsed.

Not chaotic. Not loud. Just released.

She stayed on the ground for twenty or thirty minutes. What happened in her spirit during that time is her story to tell. I only know what I witnessed. When she stood up, something had shifted.

It wasn't dramatic on the outside. But it was real. And in my heart, I heard it clear as day: "He doesn't own her anymore."

But hear me—that wasn't the beginning.

Linnie had already given her life to Jesus. She had already been saved. Salvation had already happened. But sometimes salvation is the doorway, and freedom is the walk that follows. Later, she went on her own journey called HeartQuest. Five and a half days. Five and a half days of facing wounds. Confronting lies. Inviting Jesus into the rooms of her heart, she had kept locked for years. That— she will tell you—was the true beginning of her walking in freedom.

The mountain moment confirmed it. HeartQuest deepened it.

And today? She facilitates a women's Bible study at our church. She serves in the nursery, loving babies. The same woman who once felt owned now helps other women understand they belong to Christ. Not every day is perfect. Healing still has layers. But the chains don't rattle like they used to.

And if she were sitting here on this porch with us, she would look you in the eye and say, "To those who have experienced what I experienced, you are not alone. And no matter what they say, there is a way out. Jesus can help you get out."

That's not theory. That's lived.

Freedom isn't always fireworks. Sometimes it's just a quiet truth settling deep in your soul: He doesn't own you anymore.

Jesus does.

Jim Williams

"Bear one another's burdens…"

— Galatians 6:2 (ESV)

GOAL — Get Out and Look

I kept seeing an acronym that's common in the trucking world: GOAL.

G.O.A.L. — Get Out And Look.

It's a reminder to a driver: before you back up, before you move, before you assume the path is clear — get out of the driver's seat and look. Simple. Practical. Lifesaving.

And this past Sunday, sitting in church, that acronym came back to me. I wasn't thinking about trucks. But the Lord was.

As I sat there, the thought pressed in:

This isn't just for trucking. This is for life.

When you get out and look, you have to leave the driver's seat.

How many of us are trying to follow God while still gripping the wheel? We want direction — but we don't want to surrender control.

Sometimes the most spiritual thing we can do in a busy, complicated world is simply this:

Get out of the driver's seat. Step back. Look around. Pay attention to what God is teaching in ordinary moments.

Because He's always teaching.

The day before, Austin and I had climbed in the truck and headed to Wilmington with the Smithfield car for a car show. He was excited. He wanted to walk around handing out Smithfield coupons and little pig keychains. For the younger kids, he gave away small die-cast cars.

I watched him. People just saw a kid walking up, giving things away. They didn't know his connection or his motive. He was just… a kid.

At some point, I noticed a Smithfield polo that fit him. We put him in it, along with a Smithfield cap. Something changed. He wasn't just a kid handing out items anymore. He was a representative.

He went back out and carried himself differently. Not arrogantly. Not pridefully. But confidently. He worked hard all day. And later he said:

"I had a really good time today. I actually felt like I was part of it."

Everyone wants to feel part of something. But the problem isn't the desire to belong. The problem is where we place that desire.

Many come to church hoping to belong to people. And sometimes they leave hurt. But your identity doesn't come from people — it comes from Christ. Hebrews 10:25 says not to forsake assembling together. Isaiah 61:10 reminds us:

"I will greatly rejoice in the LORD… for He has clothed me with the garments of salvation; He has covered me with the robe of righteousness…"

Clothed. Just like Austin in the polo. The Lord has dressed me in something better than a company logo — He's clothed me in salvation.

1 Peter 2:9:

"You are a chosen people, a royal priesthood, a holy nation, His own special possession."

That's identity. That's belonging. It doesn't come from the church's perfection. It comes from Christ's righteousness.

When you know you've been clothed by Christ — brought into the family — you serve differently. Not out of obligation, but because you want to.

Just like Austin.

Maybe what some of us need to do is GOAL: Get out of the driver's seat. Stop trying to control where we fit. Look around and see what God has already done.

You're not wearing the logo to prove you belong. You're wearing it because you already do. Already chosen. Already covered. Already part of the family. Now go represent your Father well.

"We weren't meant to walk this alone—

and we were never supposed to try."

— Jim Williams

The Last Thing I'll Say Tonight

If you've walked this road with me; you already know this book was never just about racing. It was about noticing. Life moves fast, and you don't get a warning before seasons change. One day, you're holding a small hand. One day, you're standing behind a casket. One day, you're chasing dreams. One day, you're rebuilding from loss.

The sparks are everywhere.

Some look like an opportunity. Some look like heartbreak. Some look like a delay. Some look like discipline. But none of them are wasted, because God wastes nothing — not the wins, not the layoffs, not the strained relationships, not the slow work of forgiveness, not the daily choosing to love someone well.

Nothing is random.

It's all shaping you.

Maybe you're standing in victory lane right now. Maybe you're sitting in the manager's office. Maybe you're staring at something broken, wondering if it can ever be restored. Wherever you are, the invitation is the same: slow down. Look around.

There are sparks in your life right now.

Pay attention to them — the loud ones, the quiet ones, even the coal that barely seems to glow. That faint ember may be the very thing that carries you through the dark.

You don't have to have everything figured out.

You just have to notice.

And when you do, you'll begin to see the thread. One day, you'll look back and realize the sparks were never accidents. They were growing. They were graceful. They were God.

The light is on.

The door is always open.

You're always welcome.

The Porch Light Is Still On

Thank you for sitting with me for a while.

For slowing down.
For thinking.
For remembering.
For wrestling with some of the things we often rush past. Life has a way of pulling us in a thousand directions.
Noise, pressure, expectations, disappointments, responsibilities…

But every now and then, we need a quiet place.
A place to breathe.
A place to reflect.
A place to be honest.

That has always been the porch for me.

Not because it's anything fancy —
but because it's where conversations happen,
where perspective returns,
where grace often feels a little easier to recognize.

If nothing else from these pages stays with you, I hope this does:

Slow down when you can.
Pay attention to what truly matters.
Extend grace to others, and to yourself.
And remember that even in complicated seasons…

Light still pushes back darkness.

And if you ever need a reminder…The porch light is still on.

Jim Williams

"If anyone would come after me,

let him deny himself and take up his cross daily…"

— Luke 9:23 (ESV)

My dearest Linnie,

As these pages close, I find myself wanting to say what matters most — not as a writer, not as a theologian, not as a man sorting through thoughts on a porch — but simply as your husband. I have written about faith, failure, redemption, and direction, and the slow reshaping of a restless heart. But if all those reflections do not lead here, then they have missed their mark.

You have walked beside me through more than anyone will ever fully know — through seasons when I stood steady, and through seasons when I came undone; through questions that did not have clean answers and growth that was slower than either of us would have preferred. If I have become a better man, it is not because time softened me. It is because God was patient — and because you were.

There were years when I did not yet understand covenant. I understood effort. I understood ambition. I understood motion. But covenant — that steady choosing, that quiet laying down of self — that lesson came slower. It came through grace I did not deserve and love that did not retreat when it could have. My love for you is not built on ease. It has been forged through refinement. It has been tested, examined, corrected, and strengthened. In that testing, it has become something steadier than feeling. It has become decision.

I do not know how many years the Lord will grant us. I have learned not to pretend I sit on heaven's planning committee. But I know this with clarity: loving you has been one of God's refining gifts in my life. If someday my voice is quiet and these words remain, let them stand without exaggeration and without regret — I loved you fully. Not perfectly. But faithfully. And where I failed, I repented. Where I faltered, I rose again. Where pride tried to linger, grace pressed it down.

If there is breath in me, it is committed to you. If there is strength in me, it is shared with you. If there is growth yet ahead,

I desire to walk into it beside you. And should the day come when one of us walks ahead into eternity before the other, do not think of absence as ending. Think of it as waiting. For the same God who carried us through wreckage, restoration, and quiet porch evenings is the God who holds what comes next.

You are not a chapter in my life. You are woven through its pages. And whatever legacy these words leave behind, let it be known that a simple man, once stubborn and wandering, learned by grace how to love steadily — and that loving you was part of that redemption.

The porch light is still on. And as long as the Lord allows me breath, my heart remains turned toward you.

Forever yours,
Jim

About the Author

Jim Williams is an author, speaker, and lifelong storyteller whose journey has carried him through a wide range of experiences — from the racetrack to the firehouse, from the mechanic's bay to riding an exceptional children's bus.

Currently enrolled at Liberty University, Jim is pursuing degrees in Biblical Studies & Theology, as well as Next Gen Ministry, with plans to continue his education in ministry.

He is an active member of Grace City Church in China Grove, North Carolina, where he serves in children's ministry and is involved in men's ministry.

Jim's writing reflects a passion for honest conversations about life, faith, struggles, growth, and the everyday moments where God often does His quietest — yet most meaningful — work.

He lives in North Carolina with his wife, Linnie. Between them, they have six children and three grandchildren.

For speaking inquiries, visit
www.porchlightreflections.com

Jim Williams

"You don't need the whole map—

just the next step."

— Jim Williams

About Porch Light Reflections Publishing

Porch Light Reflections Publishing exists to share stories of faith, redemption, marriage, and the quiet work God performs in ordinary lives.

Through books, reflections, and speaking engagements, Porch Light

Reflections seek to encourage thoughtful faith and honest conversations about the journey of life.

For more information or additional resources, visit:

www.porchlightreflections.com

Jim Williams

"Good Night"